Publishing &
Marketing
in the
Digital Age

Debbie Elicksen

Self-Counsel Press
(a division of)
International Self-Counsel Press Ltd.
USA   Canada

Self-Counsel Press acknowledges the financial support of the Government of Canada through the Canada Book Fund for our publishing activities.

Printed in Canada.

First edition: 2014

Library and Archives Canada Cataloguing in Publication

Elicksen, Debbie, author
    Publishing & marketing in the digital age / Debbie Elicksen.

Issued in print and electronic formats.

ISBN 978-1-77040-195-2 (pbk.).—ISBN 978-1-77040-952-1 (epub).—
ISBN 978-1-77040-953-8 (kindle)

    1. Electronic publishing. 2. Marketing—Data processing.
3. Rhetoric. I. Title.

Z286.E43E55 2014   070.5'797   C2014-903780-5
                                             C2014-903781-3

Foreword, permission granted by Jon Mitchell "Mitch" Jackson.

Chapter 1, interview permission granted by Aliya Leigh.

Chapter 2, Figure 8, interview and figure permission granted by Chantal Harvey and Tony Dyson.

Chapter 10, Figure 22, figure permission granted by Susy Rosado, Cynthia K. Seymour, and Lynn Ponder.

Chapter 14, Figure 42, figure permission granted by Cynthia K. Seymour.

Self-Counsel Press
(a division of)
International Self-Counsel Press Ltd.

Bellingham, WA   North Vancouver, BC
USA   Canada

Contents

Notice to Readers

Laws are constantly changing. Every effort is made to keep this publication as current as possible. However, the author, the publisher, and the vendor of this book make no representations or warranties regarding the outcome or the use to which the information in this book is put and are not assuming any liability for any claims, losses, or damages arising out of the use of this book. The reader should not rely on the author or the publisher of this book for any professional advice. Please be sure that you have the most recent edition.

Note: The fees quoted in this book are correct at the date of publication. However, fees are subject to change without notice. For current fees, please check with the court registry or appropriate government office nearest you.

Prices, commissions, fees, and other costs mentioned in the text or shown in samples in this book probably do not reflect real costs where you live. Inflation and other factors, including geography, can cause the costs you might encounter to be much higher or even much lower than those we show. The dollar amounts shown are simply intended as representative examples.

Acknowledgments

It is impossible to list everyone who has inspired and influenced me during the course of planning and writing this book. There are people mentioned and linked to for whom I have the greatest admiration. However, there are others who have held my hand in the last year and a half that I must acknowledge. Gratitude isn't a strong enough word to describe how I feel about their unwavering support.

A special shout-out to: Donna Price, Donna Matheson, Coral Sterling, Jennifer Miller-Bender, Stephen Bender, Don Henderson, Molly Henderson, Cynthia K. Seymour, Blair Sveinson, Rhonda Martin, and Steve Martin.

I also want to give a big, warm thank you to all those connected and engaging with me in all my networks. Every time I turn on my devices, I look forward to you brightening my day.

Foreword

Before Wayne Gretzky, winning at hockey was all about being stronger and faster than the other guy. All you had to do to win on the ice was to out-muscle your opponent to put the puck in the net.

Business was the same way. The large corporations would spend tens of millions of dollars in radio, television, and magazine ads to out-muscle the competition and keep everyone else out of the arena. Small- and medium-sized family run businesses rarely had a legitimate shot at competing with the bigger and stronger players.

Then along came "The Great One." Gretzky brought to hockey what the Internet and social media has brought to business. He was never the biggest, fastest, or strongest player on the ice, but by anticipating where the puck would be and approaching the game differently than everyone else he dominated and changed the game forever.

The new digital platforms now allow all of us to do business like Wayne Gretzky played hockey. No longer do we need to be the biggest or fastest players on the ice to be heard and make an impact and difference.

Social media allows almost anyone to think ahead and anticipate where the digital puck will be. With the right approach and effort, anyone can step up and be the new Wayne Gretzky of the digital world.

Before reading this book, most people will have thought of SEO as meaning "Search Engine Optimization." After reading this book, I think you'll walk away with a better understanding that what SEO really stands for is "Social Engineering Optimization." This book will show you exactly why this is the case.

The fact of the matter is that in today's world, there's a social media blur that's redefining how people do business. The difference between doing business and spending time online with social media is no longer a black and white distinction. In fact, I would argue that doing one, without the other, is often a disservice to you and your customer or client.

Today, smart people and business owners use social media to inspire, inform, educate, and build new relationships. On a personal note, using social media, my law firm has shared more free resources than ever before and this has allowed us to help thousands of people with their legal problems. Along the road, we have turned these relationships into new revenue resources and the firm has prospered. We know other lawyers and business owners who are doing the same thing. Apply the knowledge and tools in this book and you can do this too.

Want to do the same thing? Want to expand your sphere of influence like never before?

Then here's what I think you should do. Read this book. Mark it up with a yellow highlighter, fold the pages, and then read it again; take notes and, even more important, take action on the information found herein. It's important that you do this because in my opinion, if you're not onboard with the power of the Internet and embracing social media, you may not have a business to go to in five years. Get onboard or get run over. What happens next is entirely up to you.

When it's all said and done, business owners who embrace social media create happy and productive lives. These smart business owners know that the "pursuit of happiness" is an inalienable right and that it's their duty to use this right to build the best business and life possible.

In summary, I don't want you to worry about being the biggest or fastest business out there. I do want you to lace up the skates and, using the information in this book, anticipate where the puck will be in an hour, week, and year from now. Use your head and these available tools to expand your sphere of influence, build new relationships, and increase profits. Put in the work, help others, but always skate smart. Follow the coaching you'll get in this book and prosper, Gretzky-like, in business and life.

If you have any questions or comments, please feel free to reach out to me. I enjoy talking business and social and always look forward to connecting with people, just like you.

Jon Mitchell "Mitch" Jackson, Esq.
Senior Partner | Jackson & Wilson, Inc. (since 1986)
2013 California Lawyers Attorneys of the Year
JacksonandWilson.com

Preface

New developments and platforms present themselves every time you open a tab in your browser. New software, programs, media, algorithms, and search engine optimization rules — it's hard to keep up. Scratch that. It is *impossible* to stay on top of all these changes.

Shama Kabani, the author of *The Zen of Social Media Marketing*, (BenBella, 2013) said it best: "Social media changes with the speed of a tweet."

Make that: Publishing technology changes with the speed of a tweet.

There will always be room for printed books, but as newer generations take hold of the marketplace, this type of publishing will become more specialized rather than the norm.

Publishers are evolving their business practices much like the music industry reinvented theirs more than a decade ago. Today, having an Internet following and a marketing plan are every bit as important as the manuscript. A publisher likely won't sign you without it.

I live, breathe, and eat this stuff. Yet, I can never profess to know it all. By the time you learn one platform, at least five more relative sites have become live in the same breath. It can be overwhelming.

In order to learn about Internet media and how to create a following, there is no shortage of individuals who say they can help. I confirm for you: There is no such thing as a social media, technology, or publishing expert. The people who really know their stuff are the ones who play in the platforms. They are constant learners. Much of what they learn comes from participation. If they don't know the answer, they will tell you, try to find the answer, or refer you to someone who might know.

If you come across one of these social media "experts," and they don't know the names of Internet thought leaders — Guy Kawasaki, Gary Vaynerchuk, Chris Brogan, Erik Qualman, Robert Scoble — run in the opposite direction. It is the equivalent of a hockey expert not knowing the names of Wayne Gretzky, Mario Lemieux, or Sidney Crosby; or a movie expert not knowing the names of Brad Pitt, Steven Spielberg, or Meryl Streep.

A true Internet media or technology advocate and resource should not solely rest his or her laurels on one platform and dis the rest. However, though there are specialists in each of the technologies, every platform doesn't work for every audience. It is best to experiment and stick with the ones that work for you.

Don't be afraid to play, but play responsibly. Learn the platforms and how to work each to your advantage. It is your digital footprint.[1]

Some of the platform mechanics discussed in this book will undoubtedly change or disappear — probably right after I hit the send button to my publisher or before you reach the end of the page. It's unavoidable.

The information in this book is meant to be as basic as it can be so you can learn the skeleton of each media and be able to adapt with any of the changes that come through the pike. This is a book for the following people:

- Newbie: I just need to get my book on Facebook and I'm rich.

- Arm crosser: I don't do social media. It's evil. I don't need to be there.

---

1 "Digital Footprint-What Digital Footprint Are You Leaving Online?," YouTube.com, accessed July 4, 2014. https://www.youtube.com/watch?v=4P_gj3oRn8s&feature=youtu.be

- Seasoned platform user: You can't teach me anything I don't already know.

The goal is to give you a guide to help you overcome your fear of technology, understand how new publishing works, and have fun, while building your digital empire.

I tried to craft the book so it would work in concert with other Self-Counsel Press titles, including my own. This book stands alone to all the other titles, but it fills in the details of the publishing family library, namely:

- *Self-Publishing 101*, Debbie Elicksen
- *Sell Your Nonfiction Book*, Crawford Kilian
- *Writing for the Web*, Crawford Kilian
- *Marketing in the New Media*, Holly Berkley
- *Low-Budget Online Marketing*, Holly Berkley
- *The Social Media Advantage*, Holly Berkley and Amanda Walter

Before you proceed to publishing in 2014 and beyond, know this: **You are not your market.** For example, you may hate Facebook, but if that is where more than 60 percent of your target readers are, learn it, and set up a profile.

You want to write children's books for ten year olds? How are ten year olds receiving their stories? Do they use apps? Are they watching vignettes on YouTube? Are they physically picking up a print book? Look for clues as to what format you may need to publish your work.

Perhaps your audience is multigenerational or the generation is a multi-platform user. If this is the case, then consider publishing in more than one platform.

This book was created to get you to think about your readers, viewers, or listeners. It is for every creative field: writing, music, theater, film, photography, art, and whatever I missed.

A book is no longer one-dimensional. Books are no longer published. Publishing platforms have become the books. New mediums have forced us to rethink books. Today, software is media and the media is still the message.

Note: This book comes with a download available at *www.self-counsel.com/updates/publish&market/14kit.htm*, which connects you digitally to all the footnotes and sources included in this book. The download also includes access to worksheets mentioned in the book to help you stay organized while you build your social media empire.

Introduction

"Revolutions create things that are impossible."

SETH GODIN

You've got a free ticket to a stadium event, where 80 percent of the people you know are currently, and they will be staying indefinitely. Your kids are there and so are your best friends, your business colleagues, and your grandma.

At this event, everyone stays in their own chair at first. Some never move from it. Some sit there with their arms folded, and disengage. More move down an aisle when they see a couple of people they know, but they stay in their own clique — similar to high school, they don't let anyone else in. Some are like hot dog vendors: They come by the seat, interrupt the conversation to "feature dump" their product and leave, only to return every five minutes. Then there are those who know how to work the crowd, make everyone in their presence feel welcome, learn about them by striking up a conversation, which pays off for them. Everyone loves them.

You might convince yourself that you don't have to be at this event, so you refuse, mostly based on spite. You're not a lemming so you're not going to attend. Those people are crazy. They'll come around after the fad has died down, and then you can say I told you so.

You'll soon discover almost everyone you used to hang out with is still at the stadium having the time of their lives. They're getting real business done, too. However, you still refuse to go, citing all the evils that could happen because of what you've heard through trusted news sources —who are also not at the event.

Time moves on and you kind of miss those connections. They're not staying in touch. Nobody picks up a phone anymore. You're starting to feel like an outsider, peering in the window and seeing everyone have a grand time at the event. They have no intention of leaving their seats. Even if the power suddenly shuts down and leaves them in the dark, they stay, waiting until next light.

More and more people come through the turnstiles into the stadium. They stay like everyone else.

You are having even more difficulty trying to reach people. You find a few others, who are like you and not at the event (or, not online). You arrange a meet-up with them and complain about what's happened. Nobody is engaging. Nobody connects anymore. People live online and don't talk to people anymore. The world has gone mad.

Nobody younger than 30 has ever lived without a personal computer. People who grew up with rotary phones, party lines, The Beatles, and Led Zeppelin in their prime sometimes forget that every generation past 1981 was raised with technology. The following launch dates put this statement into perspective:

- 1969: The Internet is born.

- 1971: The first email is sent.

- 1980: Cable news launches. The Cold War is over. John Lennon is killed. Nintendo is born.

- 1981: IBM markets the first personal computer to the masses. Space exploration takes off. Vehicle manufacturers introduce front-wheel drive and fuel injection.

- 1983: The first cell phone reaches the marketplace.

- 1989: The World Wide Web brings the world together electronically. The MP3 launches a new era for music.

- 1988 to 1990: DSL — high speed Internet improves our World Wide Web experience.

- 1990: Internet on cell phone opens the door for mobile everything.

- 1993: The first CD burner means more storage space for files.

- 1994 to 1995: Yahoo launches. We see the first banner ad.

- 1998: Napster, Google, and the portable MP3 player become a reality.

- 2000: The dot-com bubble creates companies operating on air.

- 2001: Wikipedia, iTunes, and the iPod are created.

- 2003: MySpace becomes the first social network en masse.

- 2004: Facebook is launched.

- 2005: The YouTube website goes live.

- 2006: We see the first online travel agencies. Google buys YouTube. Facebook goes mainstream. We are introduced to Twitter and the Wii.

- 2007: Kindle, Google books, and iPhone forever change our future.

- 2008: The Barak Obama presidential campaign changes the face of marketing. MacBook Air launches.

- 2009: Angry Birds and Foursquare enter the scene. Barnes & Noble introduces the Nook.

- 2010: The Apple tablet, 3D plasma TV, and Google TV reposition how we receive our media in the future.

- 2011: Asus Eee Pad Transformer, BlackBerry PlayBook, Kindle Fire, and Google+ add to our media options.

- 2012: Samsung Galaxy SIII takes over the smartphone market.

- 2013: Smartwatch — Internet on your wrist. Snapchat introduces temporary media. Wearable technology, such as Google Glass, becomes the next best thing. Cars and toys can be created using 3D printers.

Nearly two generations have grown up without knowing a non-digital world.

Generation X was raised on Madonna, Michael Jackson, Queen, glam metal, and hair bands; the Brat Pack, *Star Wars*, MTV, cable TV, HBO, and video games too. Millennials were raised on Lady Gaga, Justin Bieber, Eminem, tablets, smartphones, and e-readers. You might even call this group the "Click and Tap Generation." A large percentage of Baby Boomers and their parents have also embraced technological changes.

While different studies cite conflicting numbers, all reports show the tablet is surging in sales, while desktops and laptops are seeing softer sales numbers. The tablet and smartphone revolutionized communications.

The Internet is where we find our news, how we research, provides us with a "paper" trail, is our playground, showcases our businesses, and has changed our lifestyle. It has replaced the telephone book and glove compartment map. If you ever want to test this theory, just ask any seven-year-old where the phone book or roadmaps are located!

1. The Internet Has Made Us Global

At the end of high school, I developed a friendship with a girl from New York (Sharon) via another girl from Boston (Mary), whom I met through the pen pal section of a monthly hockey magazine. We stayed in touch over the years through written letters, and exchanged face-to-face visits a couple of times.

On September 11, 2001, I was at a breakfast meeting in Calgary, Alberta, when the terror attacks took place at the World Trade Center. A fellow's spouse called to inform us what had happened and we congregated to watch a glimpse of it on the hotel lobby television.

I got into my car to head home, thinking about my mentor Stan Fischler in New York, knowing he was probably safe, although I was still worried. The Pentagon had already been hit by then. En route, I did manage to reach Stan's office by cell phone, and it was confirmed he was okay.

Mid-travel, the radio announced a plane crashed outside of Pittsburgh — where Sharon from New York was now living. It seemed remote that she would be at risk, but still, the thought terrified me. I tried to keep it together as I headed home. I ran in the door and grabbed the phone. It sounded a busy signal instead of a dial tone. There was no getting through to anyone. I kept trying and trying, desperate to reach her. Then I looked at my computer. It was extremely unlikely that I could reach anyone online if I couldn't get through on the phone, but I tried it anyway.

The email was sent, and within about two minutes, I received Sharon's reply. I thanked God for this wonderful miracle called technology. We exchanged emails for the next hour, which comforted me greatly.

Today, we are still in touch but find each other now through Facebook. Mary from Boston is also one of my Facebook connections, and we exchange communication at least weekly. We even watch awards ceremonies and football games together by commenting on an ongoing thread on one of our Facebook walls.

This digital communication feels much more personal than it did through letters and infrequent telephone calls because I can physically see them every time I turn on my computer. I can keep up to date on what is happening in their lives through their posts and pictures without having to ask them.

2. Business Development Is Still Conducted with Boots on the Ground, Sort Of

"Business is like cooking. Sometimes it bombs."

KIM DUKE[1]

When you create an online presence, your business is no longer local. Every campaign is global. For example, if your cupcake factory is in Rosebud, Saskatchewan, and your delicious creations spread through digital word-of-mouth to the extent that you are now getting several orders a day from as far away as India, you may want to revamp your business plan to include international orders. (That would be a *good* problem to have!)

---

1 Sales Divas, accessed July 4, 2014. www.salesdivas.com

On the Internet, content is king. Post good stuff and it might spread like a good cupcake. There are no guarantees, but if your content is bad, you'll be the only one reading it. If it's really terrible and offensive, sometimes it goes viral because people can't believe you posted it and will share it with their friends. That kind of viral isn't creating disciples.

Technology has made us connect more, but it hasn't dissipated what we have to do for business development. It is because of the ease of its use that we tend to multitask more and make more connections. Thus decision-makers are harder to reach. They may only answer the phone for people they already know. Unless you're still having a lot of success with it, cold calling by telephone may not work as well as it used to. It is more disruptive than digital communications, and your story better be smooth and to the point if you want to have any hope of getting the appointment.

Jill Konrath's book *Snap Selling*[2] (Portfolio, 2010) describes how to navigate the hurry-up sales tactics, get to the point, convey what you have to say, and ask for the close in five minutes or less. Even though people are busy and have less time to be subjected to schmoozing, salesmanship 101 still applies.

Selling has become more of a combined effort, using Internet tools to cull information, follow up, confirm, and share documents. Transactions are so global now that you never have to leave your home office computer for a face-to-face call thanks to Skype and other video conferencing sites.

Direct selling is a delicate dance on the Internet. What may look all right and even work in an email will have red and yellow blinking lights in social networks and read "Spam! Spam! Spam!"

Write well, or at least better than everyone else. The Internet has opened new platforms to share a message and promote your business, but that is not an excuse to put literacy on the shelf. If anything, you make a stronger impression if you take the time and effort to be a better writer by rereading and *editing* what you write. There is no excuse for stepping away from grammar, punctuation, and especially spelling. Figure 1 shows a news report that should have said "Armstrong used drugs" but someone wasn't on top of his or her job that day!

2 "SNAP Selling," Jill Konroth.com, accessed July 5, 2014.
  www.jillkonrath.com/snap-selling

Figure 1

REPORT: ARMSTRONG USED RUGS

Source: www.charlesapple.com/2013/01/another-embarrassing-tv-typo, accessed July 5, 2014.

3. Spam Isn't Just Another Monty Python Skit

What has increased dramatically with the Internet and social media is spamming and self-promotion. These out-of-touch marketers use these platforms in the same way as they would use traditional advertising. Elaine Lindsay of TROOL Social Media[3] calls this "spray and pray." Spread to as many people as you can and maybe you'll get a 1 percent return on investment. What it really gets you is deleted and reported as a spammer to the website host.

Digital communicators repel interruption advertising. Email marketing may still be relevant with some businesses, but the pop-up box on a website that forces someone to sign up before he or she continues is getting more annoying by the click. Know that unless a person has signed up for a newsletter, it usually heads straight to the spam folder. So, too, do those "Dear Sir, my name is Sergio and I noticed your website is not ... I can fix that" emails —right alongside the "Dearest Beloved" Nigerian scam emails.

There is one rule of thumb in digital marketing you can take to the bank. If it makes you mad when people do it to you, don't do it to other people.

4. Zip It to Me

The newspaper industry has had a difficult time fitting in. Paywalls, which prevent Internet users from accessing web page content without a paid subscription, have not worked and neither have pop-up ads in mobile. Add that not every outlet is making itself easy to be shareable.

Being shareable is extremely important to the digital community. If people like what they read, they want to spread it around.

---

3 TROOL Social Media, accessed July 5, 2014.
   http://troolsocial.com/2013/08/elaine-lindsay%E2%99%A0linkedin-requests-%E2%99%A6-timely-tip

This is how stories go viral. Hits and clicks are the new currency. You *want* your content shared. The more people who like you enough to share your content, the more it is shared, the more disciples you create, and the more opportunity you have to convert them into paying clients or customers. See Figure 2 for an example of what not to do. You want people to share your information on places like Pinterest.

Figure 2

Source: www.calgarysun.com

Internet rules 101:

- Don't plan to be viral; instead, post good information.

- Serve the on-demand society or people will go somewhere else.

- Make it accessible. Paywalls, forcing visitors to watch Flash messaging, and any other hostage-holding tool will push people to the next site.

- Make it mixable. Use transmedia to tell the story on different platforms.

- Make it shareable.

5. From Analog to Digital

In dictionary terms, analog represents continuous electrical frequency. Digital means continuous wave signals.

When I think of analog, I think of the old school mentality that is rigid, unwavering, closed-minded, and stuck in position —similar to a box. I call the old way of doing things "analog." That means doing things the same way because it has always worked that way in the past. Digital is more like a ball that keeps rolling forward. (See Figure 3.)

Figure 3

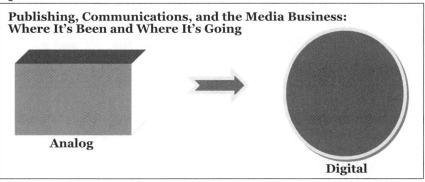

There is an element of the buying public that will always want to feel print, but that demographic is shrinking. Print is expensive. It's eco-unfriendly. It takes too long, and the information may be outdated before it gets into your hands.

In traditional media (e.g., TV, radio, newspaper), a public relations firm, a company, or an author tries to convince a reporter or editor that he or she has a product, business, or story worthy of writing about. The premise is that no one will hear about you unless the media makes it possible.

Enter 2010 and the age of the e-reader and tablet. Everyone is a publisher. Couple that with social media and everyone is the media. You can directly reach your personal audience — followers who are automatically interested in what you have to say.

Whether you are analog (old school) or digital (new school) there are principles of marketing and publishing that do *not* change. The first thing you have to remember about marketing is nobody gives a rat's behind about your product, service, or book.

People want to know what's in it for them. For example, say a person walks up to you at a networking event and says, "Hey, you should buy my book. It will help you discover the meaning of life. It's about my life story. It's also a recipe book for hemp." Yeah, you'll get right on that, won't you? You probably won't bother to answer the person, and instead, try to shrink away, hoping he or she doesn't see you again as you stroll through the venue.

Unfortunately, that's how most people market. They do it the same, whether analog or digital. They make assumptions. They don't pay attention to who their market is. They "product dump" in front of as many breathing humans as they can find. It wasn't an effective way to market in 1989, and it doesn't work today.

6. Assumptions Are Sales Killers

When telephone solicitors call me and say, "Hello Mrs. Elicksen," I don't care if they are selling a guaranteed date with Brad Pitt for $1; they lost me at hello. Don't assume and don't insult. To me, that is like saying, "Are you the little lady of the house? Oh, great. Is your husband home?"

This brings me to a real phone call I made to a sports collectible shop. I'm an avid sports collector and every so often, I purge some of my collection to make room for new stuff. The shop owner I contacted was well known in the collectible business. Although I hadn't dealt with him before, I knew his name and his reputation. I mentioned the several boxes of hockey and baseball cards I wanted to sell; some of them were valuable rookie cards that went back to the 1960s. I wanted to see if he was in the marketplace for them and if I could arrange a meeting. His response was, "Does your husband know you are selling his collection?" Needless to say, I gave him a blunt remark, hung up the phone, and found another dealer —whom I'm sure made at least a few thousand dollars on the resale.

Not everyone is interested in what you have to offer. Not even free gasoline without any strings attached. What if he or she doesn't drive a car? Or, maybe it's a hybrid? Target the right people and position the right message. Many factors go into a successful marketing launch.

Targeted and strategic methods are more effective than fast and easy. Yet most people choose fast and easy, especially on the Internet, and then wonder why these efforts are not paying off.

Salespeople are created in childhood. For example, you learned how to sell at an early age when you whined and pleaded for that pet or toy at age three, when you convinced your friend to ride his bike into that field with the "no trespassing" sign, and when you shook the Pounce tin to lure the cat back into the house. All these activities are a form of salesmanship because they offer something the target market wants. For example, "I'll stop whining if you get me a rabbit." (That actually did work on my dad.) "It will be fun," (with the element of adrenaline to not get caught trespassing). And the cat came in the house because she knew I would give her a treat.

In the early days of my career, when I found an advertising position that suited me, I became a student of the craft. In those days, you used the library to research, so I checked out every book I could find on advertising and marketing. I'd look for creative ideas on ads and campaigns. I paid attention to the ads I noticed, then I would go back and look at the ads I missed and evaluate why. I created a bad ad file for the advertisements that would insult the reader, such as Figure 4.

Figure 4

Source: RE/MAX print advertisement

I might have carried the title of an ad rep but I acted like an advertising agency on wheels. It was more than just an ad; it had to fit the company branding, business, vision, and purpose. I wanted to get the whole picture of the business so I could help the design people create an effective ad and maybe create a long-term account.

That's a similar approach you can use with your own digital media campaign. Be a student — a consistent learner.

7. Good Marketing Meets the Internet

When you look at how the publishing industry is evolving and how social networks have grown and influenced our world, advertising that is worthy gets pushed out virally to even more people than the advertiser initially expected or paid for.

Volkswagen is a great example.[4] Weeks before the 2011 Super Bowl an ad was prelaunched on YouTube that went viral overnight to the tune of about 1 million. The day after the game, the views more than doubled. Today the ad keeps growing in hits. As of April, 2014, the hits were at 59,697,133.

While traditional paid advertising used to hit the mainstream market via newspapers, radio, and television, what companies would die for was the unpaid advertising; the kind where a reporter decided to do a story on a company based on its press release.

In the larger centers, the competition was (is) stiff. It is not unusual for reporters to receive more than 150 press releases per day. Because they receive so many, they take a glance at the title and maybe the first sentence, and if that information doesn't pique the reporters' interest, zap, it's gone.

Today, if you advertise your business in a mainstream newspaper, chances are nobody younger than 40 will see your ad, unless it is a pop-up ad on the Internet. This makes it all the more critical that you know who your target audience is.

8. People Want It Here and They Want It Now

The 24-hour news cycle means if it happened a second ago, we expect a report in less than five minutes. In reality, when something happens, a news station is still trying to assess the story and assign a reporter.

---

4 "The Force," YouTube.com, accessed July 4, 2014. www.youtube.com/watch?v=R55e-uHQnao

The more cutbacks and folding companies in the publishing and media business, the less relevance paid journalists have when it comes to spreading the news.

Nobody wants to wait five hours to learn about an incident in their neighborhood. As mainstream media scrambles to catch up with the story, or at least post it online, frustrated readers turn to their friends on Facebook and ask the question in their status updates, "Does anyone know what happened?" Or they go to Twitter and use the keyword finder to hunt down tweets from the people who were at the scene. People will tweet about it play-by-play. That is real-time news, on the scene, as it happens. It may not be entirely accurate or verifiable, but they get the sense of the situation long before the media assigns a reporter. Then, as has been known to happen, the reporter might even use the information in the tweets to fill out his or her story.

This method of citizen journalism is here to stay (e.g., CitizenTube on YouTube.com). It's the only way we can get a story in situations where media is banned, such as the volatile uprisings in the Middle East.

Because of cameras in our cell phones, we can take onsite video and post it to YouTube or CNN iReport in minutes. We are the media now.

So it's no surprise that the book publishing industry is evolving, too. There will always be those who like hard copy publications, but it's much easier to carry books inside a Kindle.

The future is exciting! The opportunities, the creative options, and the ability to connect one-on-one with the audience are where it's at.

You don't have to rely entirely on mainstream media to push your message via paid and unpaid advertising. You are the media and you are the publisher. You are connected to your audience directly. You can create a community of not just like-minded people, but people who are intriguing, who have an interest in you, who help you spread your message, buy your book, and who engage you with compelling content, advice, and entertainment. It's totally awesome. Let me show you how it's done.

1
Content Creation

"Writing a book is a horrible, exhausting struggle, like a long bout of some painful illness. One would never undertake such a thing if one were not driven on by some demon whom one can neither resist nor understand."

GEORGE ORWELL

Books are like babies. When it's yours, you're all gaga over it, and you show everybody its picture and tell them what a great book it is, and you think everyone will want to hold it. What you don't see is that your target victims are putting on a fake smile, saying, "Oh yes, it's so sweet" but what they are thinking is it looks the same as every other book. They're so not that into it, and they are desperately scoping the scene for an easy getaway.

It is okay that you love your baby. It's okay to be proud. You should be. Even your target victims will agree to that. Just don't assume everyone in your path is a fan.

When you decide to write a book or blog, create a video or audio file, or update your Facebook status — always have a purpose in mind. Everything you craft should lead to an overall intention. If that is still unclear, ask yourself:

- Who are you?

- Who do you want to be?

- What do you want to be known for?

- What is your mission or goal?

- How do you want people to feel when they follow you?

- What makes your heart sing?

If you can't answer who you are, and what your vision is, you can best be described by other people within your trusted circles. What do they say about you? They see what is in your heart. That is what you should focus on.

In the late 1990s and early 2000s, I worked with city newspapers writing advertising features. This type of work could be called selling businesses on paper. The goal was that once the readers finished reading the piece, they'd jump into their vehicles and drive to the establishment to purchase the item featured in the article.

Writing advertising features is really copywriting. Selling "on paper" is also something you do when you write a press release, book cover, pitch letter, or website copy. It is something every author or businessperson should learn how to do.

There was a perception in the newsroom that if you wrote for the section that did advertising features, you were incapable of writing editorial (i.e., news and other section articles). For a career in media, you had to choose between advertising and editorial. Of course, I bucked the system because I learned both. To say that a copywriter cannot write editorial or an editorial writer can't write ad copy is like saying you can either write nonfiction or fiction, and you can only write about one topic for the rest of your life. Or if you're an actor, you are not allowed to direct or produce. Tell that to Angelina Jolie, Clint Eastwood, Ron Howard, and Penny Marshall.

You are not the sum of your job. You are more than a mother, father, sister, nationality, or religion. You can be more than one thing at the same time or you can be one thing. You can write about more than one topic — and you should. You can write more than one genre. Most important, learn how to write for more than one platform.

1. Spreadable Storytelling

Writing a blog is different than writing a white paper. Writing a tweet is different than creating a Google+ post or a Facebook update. All of these can be made into snippets to lead to a bigger story that fits your purpose. For example, all of these things can be used for materials for a book.

Creating great content is about finding an idea that people want to read, see, or hear. You want to create something so contagious that everyone in your target audience will want to share it.

Write down every idea that seems viable at the time. Keep a notepad handy in every room of your home so you can catch the ideas as soon as they come out of your mind. Transfer the idea from the notepad into a notebook, an MS Word document, or put it into your email draft folder (I use this when I want to quickly save something with easy access), or use Evernote, Google Drive, or another type of cloud storage. Use a tape recorder, video camera, or another form of media to fine-tune your editorial direction.

Mark Zuckerberg used handwritten journals to jot down notes about how he wanted Facebook to grow and included ideas from other thought leaders about how they excelled in their businesses.

I use handwritten notebooks to cull key points from great thinkers; to bullet-point my research; and to take notes from interviews, movies, commercials, and whatever else might spawn an idea. I also type some of these notes (the ones that stand out the most) into a Google Drive document and store it on the Web. Create and save your ideas in a way that feels right for you.

Only 1 in 1 billion posts actually goes viral. Truthfully, I just plucked that statistic out of the air, but there is a very strong chance that your topic is not unique. There will be endless sources and links where people can find the same message. What gets their attention is what *they* perceive as the best value. Value can come in great literary skills, but that can't be your sole feature. When the words possess the power to move hearts and souls, then it becomes spreadable.

Your videos do not have to be professionally done, but they should have an element of professionalism and show that you are real. I came across two great examples. They relate to and tap into a heavily favored demographic: youth. These people created a brand from their own selves:

- With more than 2 million subscribers, IISuperwomanII[1] is so popular, there is a second YouTube channel: SuperwomanVlogs.[2] What Kids Really Mean[3] shows you her appeal. She is also a very smart marketer. Her YouTube channels and social media sites are her websites, and yes, she sells merchandise, too.

- Marc Guberti[4] is a teenage digital content creator who is just getting his feet wet. He does have a dedicated website[5] besides his digital media sites, and at 16, he had written four books, among other things.

Both Superwoman and Guberti schedule their posts to appear at the same time in the same place every week. They are consistent in their messaging. They provide an element of professionalism in their videos.

Good content will not go viral overnight. It takes a long time to get people to come after you build it. It doesn't matter what you like, because if the public doesn't like it, it dies where you left it.

Find a network and make it your own. If you like Twitter, craft tweets that push people to think. Make that your *modus operandi*.

Being spreadable means just that. You can't hog and hold all of your stuff and expect that people will pay for it unless the content is outstandingly unique — and even then you still need to offer more value. See how well those paywalls are working for the newspaper industry.

If you provide really great links and posts, people will keep returning for more content. There is no greater feeling in the world than when a stranger thinks highly enough of your blog entry to share it with his or her followers or retweets your tweet.

This doesn't mean that if you write a book — like this one — you have to give it away. What you do is take snippets of it. For

1 IISuperwomanII, YouTube.com, accessed July 5, 2014. www.youtube.com/user/IISuperwomanII
2 Superwoman Vlogs, YouTube.com, accessed July 5, 2014. www.youtube.com/user/SuperwomanVlogs
3 "What Kids Really Mean," YouTube.com, accessed July 5, 2014. http://youtu.be/v7upXtporew
4 Marc Guberti, YouTube.com, accessed July 5, 2014. www.youtube.com/user/MarcGuberti
5 Marc Guberti, MarcGuberti.com, accessed July 5, 2014. http://marcguberti.com/

example, the first sentence in this paragraph can be a tweet. This whole paragraph can be LinkedIn text added to a link to the Self-Counsel Press website page that features this book. I can do the same in Facebook. In Google+ I can actually take a segment and make a blog post from it, post it to my own blog and then add the link to the Self-Counsel page.

However, you would not do this type of content on every post. The next post could be in YouTube: A one-minute commentary discussing one of the segments in this chapter. That YouTube post can be linked to Google+ and show up there, too. Then, add information into the description that would include the link to where people can buy the book.

Do not make your posts all about you. Spread other people's messages, links, and information. Post tips, yes, but when you promote your book, do it sparingly. You would have your book information on your digital media profile so if someone consistently likes what you are sharing across the board, he or she can click on your profile and learn more about you.

2. Be Consistently Good

Being consistently good won't happen overnight. Everything is a process. Work in a platform that is comfortable for you. If you love to write, always wanted to be a writer, or you're afraid to write but think you have to — then write. Don't wait for a perfect moment or a perfect day for this and that to get done. Writers write, period. They procrastinate, too, but ultimately, they get off their duffs and tap their thoughts into a keyboard. It all begins with an idea.

If you like playing a guitar and singing, learn how to use YouTube. Post a cover song if the music belongs to someone else or post an original song with lyrics.

Interview someone to create a podcast. Or if you're ambitious and serious about scheduling, develop your own radio show.

My cohost Cynthia K. Seymour[6] and I created Virtual Newsmakers[7], a web video show that airs weekly on Google+ Hangouts on Air, where we interview guests who are bridging traditional and digital communications.

6 Cynthia K. Seymour, Google+, accessed July 5, 2014. https://plus.google.com/+CynthiaKSeymour/about
7 Virtual Newmakers, YouTube.com, accessed July 5, 2014. www.youtube.com/user/VirtualNewsmakers/videos

We use YouTube as our main website, and we developed social media pages in Facebook, Twitter, Google+, and Pinterest. We also converted some of our YouTube videos to an MP3 format and edited them into podcasts, which we uploadeded via PodOmatic to iTunes.[8]

Our high-profile guests include thought leaders in digital media, such as Erik Qualman and Chris Brogan; celebrities such as Olympian bobsledder Steve Mesler and R2D2 creator Tony Dyson; and everyday people doing interesting stuff in digital media. We covered a variety of topics from gamifying your television to rhino poaching in South Africa. Overall, the goal is to bring in guests who fit the editorial guideline, and we ask them to provide tips and a challenge of the week to our viewers.

Even though Cynthia and I had a decent following in digital media to start, building an audience for Virtual Newsmakers didn't happen overnight. It took consistent effort and because this was two women creating and promoting a show from our living rooms, we took pleasure in the smallest of victories — reaching 100 subscribers on YouTube, HuffPost Live doing a shout-out of our show (see Figure 5), and adding a new continent to our broadcast locations.

Figure 5

3. What Should You Create?

If a 100- or 200-page book seems too daunting and expensive to print, consider other options to make yourself look like an authoritative voice or to get your story out.

---

8 Virtual Newsmakers on iTunes, iTunes.com, accessed July 5, 2014. https://itunes.apple.com/ca/podcast/virtual-newsmakers/id766097442

People love white papers. This is where you can write about trends, industry problems, a history of something, a solution, benefits of a product, or some sort of information that is tip-filled and valuable to the readers. White papers are free reports meaning free content that is usually of a length that isn't too onerous to read. A lot of companies use white papers to capture readership data by asking readers to complete an online form in order to download the report. If the report is full of great ideas, the readers will willingly submit their information to see future content that is produced. If they read your white papers over time, they might take an interest in what your company produces. Call it free advertising without being interruptive. The key to a good white paper is that it offers some of your best ideas, doesn't give away the farm, and it doesn't sell. White papers are blog posts on steroids.

Blogs sell but they don't use selling language or direct language such as "buy my stuff." Rather they provide a platform for you to shine with your authoritative voice. Blogs should be selfless, like the white paper. Blogs don't have to be text-driven. You can use photographs, audio, and video to share your expertise or talk about someone else's. There is no harm in asking your viewers to share your content at the end of your post.

Create a one-minute video blog on a trending topic, your point of view, or a tip. That video can morph into a blog post, be distributed to Google+, Twitter, and other social networks. Ideally, you would set up the link with new text in each platform so it is fresh and doesn't look like a link you just threw to the wind.

Google now uses semantic search, which means the search engine looks at the seeker's intent and the contextual meaning of content in order to match the two. It's not about keywords anymore. Gone are the days where you could drop keywords into your web pages and blog post content in order to be found.

The well-known Google "Plusser" Martin Shervington[9] and semantic search coach David Amerland[10] suggest you focus your content on answering a question, like one that would be asked in a search engine (e.g., "how do I tie a knot?"). Google looks at the value of the page. So write for your audience first, then for the search engines. In other words, be a trusted source of information.

---

9 Martin Shervington, MartinShervington.com, accessed July 5, 2014. www.martinshervington.com
10 David Amerland, DavidAmerland.com, accessed July 5, 2014. http://davidamerland.com/about/bio.html

This doesn't mean you have to always stay within your niche. It's okay to talk about other subjects; you see this in engaged communities across the web. It all boils down to what you want people to come to you for. You also find part of your audience by creating the content.

The people who consistently send group or private messages in social networks and emails asking people to share their content — which is clearly not aligned with the receiver's taste — may work against the creator and get Google to discount the content. Consider Google like Big Brother. It knows everything; what you see, think, and feel. Because all of its platforms are tied together, and other networks show up in it, it sees the content that is true to your likes. It also knows when you are sharing nonaligned content. Google owns the world, we just play in it, and we get better mileage if we play by its rules.

4. When All Else Fails at Getting a Publisher, Do It Yourself

Aliya Leigh is a digital media producer, author, and blogger from Phoenix, Arizona. She owns a production and publishing company that focuses on independent films, web shows, and graphic novels. She is the author of two novels: *Mystery* (Aliya Leigh, 2010) and *Cyber Pirates* (Aliya Leigh, 2011).

She became her own media and production company after having some difficulty in getting a publishing agent. She hired a public relations person to help her, thinking that if she received more exposure, it would help with her portfolio, and ultimately help her get an agent. She did get some exposure, but not enough to bring her an agent.

Leigh took matters into her own hands and learned as much as she could about social media; she took some classes, then set up profiles on the main platforms and began her quest to create a following.

Leigh says, "One of the biggest exposures I got was my podcasts, which I did for five years. I used libsyn.com. It's a syndicated blog."

When you get more popular with a podcast, and you have the numbers to prove it, Leigh suggests talking to the host to see if it will help fund you by getting you ads. That's how she was able to get paid to do her podcast. Once you get big, company sponsors become easier to find.

Her books are grounded in personal experience. Leigh says, "*Mystery* is based on my aunt's death. She dealt with domestic violence and was killed. [The book] is about a woman who finds love again after she's dead."

Gathering exposure for the book was difficult. Another aunt suggested she do an audiobook. Because Leigh had just gone through a breakup, it seemed like a perfect platform for her to talk about the emotions that come with that. It turned into her podcast.

"*Cyber Pirates* was actually my first, but I got so much grief writing that book. I had joined the Horror Writers Association, and they never liked it. They said it was terrible, it was awful; I don't know why you wrote this book. So I put it on the backburner and just kept with *Mystery* and published that first."

Once everyone knew her from the podcast and she now had exposure, she published *Cyber Pirates*. "That book deals with my love of hacking. I used to be a hacker back in the days when I was a computer programmer — also my love of *Sims* [life simulation video game]. The book was developed by *Sims*. I'm a big-time gamer."

Her web series *Mercy Me* is based on a true story. "My grandmother died of anorexia. She was 86 years old and wanted a mercy killing [which was not available to her] because eventually her body stopped functioning. I was in Arizona and all my family were in New York. They called me by phone and asked, 'Can you please hear your grandmother die?' I spoke to her in her final hours and told her, 'Just let go and move on.' It was really touching, but at the same time, it was heartbreaking to do that. After I did that and hung up the phone, 30 minutes later, she died. It hurt me, so I decided to write a story about it."

Mercy Me is about a mercy-killing doctor who displays no emotion. Leigh wrote the blog first, and at the end of it, discussed how the character had to kill her grandmother because she had stage-four cancer. The series continued with the character's internal discussion: "I killed my grandmother. I don't know if I should continue practicing or not."

Mercy Me morphed into an animated web series. "With the animation, I wrote the story. From there, I was trying to sell it to studios because I wrote the script for it, too. My friend, who is actually the voice of Mercy, told me I could do it myself."

Leigh did her own animation using anime (Japanese animated productions that are usually hand-drawn or computer animations). The software she used to create anime is Anime Studio.[11]

She has thought about changing *Cyber Pirates* into animation for educational purposes.

"I'm also planning on writing another book called the *Pi Equation*, an adult book that deals with how life will be in the future. If there was a type of mathematical equation that everyone lived by, how would we all develop and be in society? Because we have a credit score — so think about that credit score being your life."

Through her journey of publishing her own content, Leigh discovered she loves podcasting and animation, especially Japanese anime. Everything she did cost her zero dollars.

5. The New Hard Copy

I spent one and half years in physical transition, conducting business exclusively from my computer devices. My face-to-face meetings were in Skype and private Google+ Hangouts. Without access to a printer, I saved emails and web documents as PDFs (portable document formats) on a device or in the cloud (Internet storage). Lugging books was not an option, so my Kindle carried them for me. It is now a way of life.

It may seem like there is a parallel universe between the traditionalists and the digital community. Communications have been digital for years. Unless you still use a typewriter, a rotary phone, a television with rabbit ears, and drive a vehicle older than one from 1988, you may think you are living as a traditionalist, but the world around you has become digital. For example, television broadcasts officially switched from analog to digital in 2009 (in the US).

Offset printing presses receive files digitally. There is no such thing as typesetting anymore. All publishing is communicated to the press digitally. That means the only way you can publish your handwritten book is to photocopy it as a book or scan it so

---

11 Anime Studio, accessed July 5, 2014. http://anime.smithmicro.com/

it can become a digital image. There is no way of getting around it. Your book needs to be in electronic files if you want to have it published. Only under special circumstances would a publisher accept a manuscript in handwritten form.

Layout people need the raw manuscript in a Microsoft Word (or similar) document. It is the universal software that can be converted into other software programs. A PDF cannot be manipulated, although a graphic designer can play with it to a certain extent if he or she has Adobe software.

You can create and publish your book in MS Word, but trust me, it's a royal pain in the keister. It seems every time you breathe on the file, even open it up, it moves! That means you are constantly lining up the text, moving photos to the right spot, and making sure the headers are in the right place. After about ten times of doing this, expect to chastise yourself: Why didn't I hire a graphic designer?

Because digital presses have improved a lot over the last few years, an MS Word document turns out all right when the file is used to publish from. You just won't be able to use it for an offset press, unless you don't care how bad your book turns out. It may turn out badly anyway if you didn't check it one last time before saving it into a PDF. That is how the printer wants to receive the files it uses regardless of the type of printing press.

If you leave the book in an MS Word document and add some sort of cover page to it, you can save it as a PDF, and voilà! You have what is known as an eDoc. You can sell it as a download file.

The same PDF can be converted into a MOBI file (i.e., Kindle book), an EPUB file, or any other electronic version of an ebook. It's not always easy to find someone who can do this. Graphic designers still want to maintain their position in print books, it seems, but now Kindle allows you to convert your book for free. Other programs will likely sprout up very soon, in which you can make all your conversions simply and for free.

6. Organize Your Thoughts

Everybody operates differently. If the end result is the same, it probably doesn't matter how you get there. You need to figure out what works best for you. A good place to start is by creating a table of contents to help you organize the flow of your book.

You may already have some text mulling in your brain that is itching to get out, so write it down and file it for later. Keep a physical notebook (I use several) handy to jot down research notes or whatever comes to your head so you can reference it later.

You may find it easier to stay organized by keeping your writing in Evernote, a Word document, or a Google Drive file. Or, by using a video recorder, web cam, or tape recorder.

There are numerous places to store your research besides a brick and mortar location. You can keep your research organized by bookmarking websites, blog entries, and other pertinent information you find on the Web.

You might have a better way or a process that works for you, but let me tell you how I put this book together: folders. I broke down each chapter into its own folder, or MS Word document (see Figure 6). The folder of the same name housed images I could attribute to the chapter. In each MS Word document (chapter), I copied and pasted information from interviews, prior text I had written, blog posts, and web articles. In order to separate my work from the research, I used a different font. When I returned to the Word document to write the chapter, any of the interview material that was edited, I changed the font into my material font, and then went onto the next task.

Figure 6

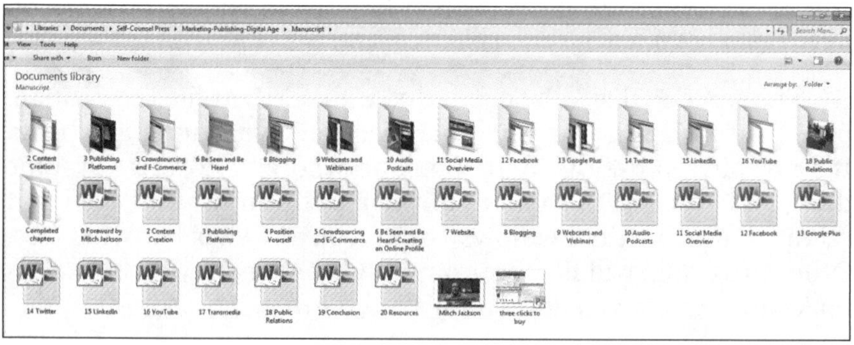

Even when you think the research is done, there is more to look up once you start crafting the words. I also added screenshots as I went along. The biggest challenge is to remember all the research you cull.

The notes were copied and pasted right into the appropriate MS Word document. I put all I could muster onto the page, saved it, and then tackled writing the book one chapter at a time.

This process may work differently for fiction books. There, you have characters to consider, but you could use a similar process to keep track of a character's developments and details. I believe many fiction authors use a spreadsheet. You can have one in Google Drive you can access from anywhere. It is especially handy if you don't have Windows Office (for Excel) in your computer.

Once a chapter was deemed relatively complete, I transferred it into a new folder for edited content. Then I inserted and combined those edited chapters into a main MS Word document. That didn't mean I was done. Editing is an ongoing process. You know you're done when you get sick of looking at it to the point of nausea or after a couple of rounds of very minor changes, then you have to give yourself permission to give it up.

7. If You Can't Create Content on Your Own, Partner with Someone

Aliza Sherman and Danielle Smith are coauthors of the bestselling books: *Mom Incorporated* (Sellers Publishing Inc., 2011) and *Social Media Engagement for Dummies* (For Dummies, 2013). Smith is a video correspondent, spokesperson and speaker, and publisher of ExtraordinaryMommy.com and DanielleSmithMedia. com. Sherman is a web pioneer — a social media and mobile evangelist, international speaker, blogger, podcaster, and has authored nine books. Learn more in their Virtual Newsmakers interview.[12]

The two women have coauthored their two books virtually — a collaboration that began when Sherman was approached by a publisher following her eighth book.

Sherman says, "We brainstormed ideas and came up with *Mom Incorporated*. I happened to have reserved "Mom Incorporated" years ago as a domain name. I thought telling a story about starting a business from home would be interesting and helpful. I was brain dead from writing my other book and asked: Is it possible for me to have a coauthor? Then I thought, who do I know who writes really well, has a warm voice, and truly understands

12 Virtual Newsmakers featuring Aliza Sherman and Danielle Smith, YouTube.com, accessed July 5, 2014. www.youtube.com/watch?v=U2ojBbSTpZs

what it's like to be a mom in business, and I thought of Danielle. So I messaged her."

The two had only met at a couple of conferences, but Sherman remembered Smith and thought she would be a good fit for a writing partner. She sent Smith a Facebook message, "Do you have a book deal lined up, and if you don't, do you want one?"

What Sherman didn't know was that Smith had always thought about writing a book. She was just a little surprised that it would come about this easily. Of course, she responded yes.

Both writing styles are completely different but their collaboration worked well. Smith's style was more free-flowing and conversational, and she added warmth to the book. Sherman's approach was analytical, intelligent, witty, and with more of a business structure.

How it worked was they traded off chapters. Sherman wrote one chapter; Smith wrote another. Then they traded chapters with each other. One would straighten out the text and the other would soften it up. Eventually their voices melded the book.

When Smith's husband read it, he offered a huge compliment — he couldn't always tell which writing belonged to which author. However, the women could always tell.

Virtual tools made it easier to collaborate, and especially to conduct interviews. They did everything virtually with the book. They worked with Google documents, MS Word documents, and Skype calls. They did finally meet up for book tours.

Sherman and Smith had a rhythm down pat from the first book when the second book materialized, but this writing process was different. The first book, *Mom Incorporated*, was their idea in which they interviewed more than 80 women about their stories and advice. The second book, *Social Media Engagement for Dummies*, was more difficult because they had a specific structure they had to follow from the Dummies series.

"We had to take all of our ideas and our styles and then squish them into the structure," explains Sherman. "We did it all virtually again, but it was a lot more challenging."

Smith adds, "I love that Aliza said it was a little bit harder. When, in fact, I cried. If you read the acknowledgments in the book, there is a section where I say thank you to my husband for sleeping on the floor in my office while I cried. He literally said to me, if you can do this, you can do anything. I felt at the time it was truly the most challenging thing I had ever done — fitting myself into a very specific box."

They had one editor with *Mom Incorporated* and up to six editors — in just one chapter — with the Dummies book. What made things more difficult was that sometimes the editors gave them conflicting information.

8. Maintain Your Computer Better Than Your Car

If you knew how many people I've come across who said they lost everything — their entire manuscript and all of its research because of a computer crash, blip, or virus, then you'll forgive my nagging.

First, confirm that your computer is up-to-date with its insurance: Antivirus software. If you can't afford insurance, one can be appointed for you for free via AVG. There are many choices for antivirus software, either by downloading it or installing it from a CD.

I used to swear by a specific antivirus program for years until a computer exorcist (a person who eradicates nasty demons from a device) turned me onto VIPRE Antivirus. I did some checking online for ratings and discussion boards. Discussion feeds are great for learning about any sort of quirks you can expect from software or a device. VIPRE topped the list of antivirus products. One of the things I liked was that VIPRE didn't hog space on my computer like other programs did.

Once you choose your software, make sure the settings allow for automatic updates. You don't want to have to trust yourself to do this manually.

Heed this warning: Go directly to the software manufacturer's site to download. There are websites that are a great place to go to look for product reviews, but don't use their links to download the software. What happens is a basket of cyber-baddies you don't really want could land inside your computer as part of the package. Click "no" on any callout box that wants to add a toolbar in your browser.

Antivirus programs don't protect you against everything, especially stupidity when you click a bad link on a social media site (which usually infiltrates your social media information) or a faux website by accident. For goodness' sake: Do not click any email link from PayPal, banks, Facebook, or Twitter, or any other site that seems suspicious. Not only are you asking for a virus, you are asking for someone to infiltrate your account. Go directly to the website to log in.

If you click a Twitter email link (some are legit, many are not) or that salacious looking video with the big boobs in your Facebook feed, you have likely put out a welcome mat for a predator to hold your account hostage. You're in good company if you have done this, but once you realize it, quickly jump into action.

Don't worry. This is an easy fix. Go into Twitter or Facebook, log out, log back in, and change your password. For your bank or PayPal — you're going to have to contact the companies directly. You'll know for sure something happened when your money starts disappearing, but you don't have a joint account.

Make sure your computer's security settings are at the recommended level. Go to the Control Panel to see that your firewall is turned on. A firewall is just like it sounds: It helps keep the hackers out.

8.1 Blood-sucking files

Your next step is to go into your computer settings and click "Accessories," then "System Tools," and then "Disk Cleanup." This cleans up the files that plug your computer's efficiency. Every time you click on a website page, there are cache images and files that stay on your computer, which Disk Cleanup can remove. You can also set your browser (e.g., Chrome, Firefox, Explorer) to erase the "History" every time you shut down the Internet. That history is every web page plus every image on that page you visited during the course of a day, which adds to that cache.

Use the "Disk Defragmenter" at least once a month. What this does is it removes some of the deleted files, which frees up more space.

These simple steps will help your computer run better. Not doing it will end up slowing down its performance because of all the garbage that stays stored. The more time you spend online, the more trips you have to make to the refuse bin.

8.2 Back up your files or hear me say, "I told you so"

Imagine trying to rewrite a manuscript from scratch or redoing the entire year's financial spreadsheet because it was not backed up onto any exterior drive when you clicked that faux file or website by accident, and all of a sudden, your computer is frozen and a computer exorcist has been called to clean it, while hopefully salvaging what's left on the drive. Or, the file you have almost finished creating is lost due to a small power surge.

If your computer is old (i.e., four years or older), expect it to crash. They even crash when they are new. Computers are vehicles that drive on the Internet. Don't be a drunk driver.

Back up your intellectual property. If your file is still in progress and you don't have time to save it externally, once you finish working on it for the day, back it up by emailing it to yourself. If you have a few more minutes, upload it to Google Drive or Dropbox. These are free cloud storage facilities. You can also buy a service that automatically backs up your computer to an external server at the end of the day.

Save often. Save after almost every line. You won't remember what you wrote halfway through that second line. It isn't a matter of *if* it will happen, it's *when*. Be armed and ready for the day you can no longer use your computer.

8.3 Account safety and password organization

Unless you have a photographic memory, set up a system for keeping track of your websites, user names, and passwords. You can use a spreadsheet, an MS Word doc, or anything that is easily accessible. Personally, I've used a Word document, which I would print off (16 pages) and keep beside me, and when I joined a new site, I'd handwrite the user/login on the printout and update at a later date. Yes, it is a bit archaic, and I also have the same document saved in Google Docs. In the download kit included with this book, you'll find an MS Excel Password Management file that will help you stay organized.

Don't use the same login for every account. Change some of them once in a while. Make the login hard for hackers to figure out. Don't use your kids' names or birth dates. If you have trouble figuring out a password — especially one for a site you visit often, maybe use uppercase and lowercase letters to spell out one of your rival sports teams' right fielders, including his number (e.g., hAnkAaroN#44).

Picking passwords can be a challenge. In using the player system, I'll pick a player and number from the last website I visited. Look around the room or outside your window, see an object, and add more detail to the description, for example: "BluejayEating-Millet2day."

For a user name, if that is the name that shows up in the profile, use your name as often as you can. (Hint: Your name then shows up in Google.)

2
Publishing Platforms

As you'll discover in the following chapters, there are many publishing platforms. This chapter mainly covers different forms of book publishing (i.e., ebooks and printed) but also includes information about apps, photography, music, and film.

1. Traditional Book Publishing

Many books are produced every year. Nick Morgan, a contributor for Forbes.com[1], wrote that depending on which statistics you look at, there are 600,000 to 1 million books produced every year in the United States, and at least half are self-published. Most self-publishers sell fewer than 250 copies.

Bowker[2] is the supplier for American ISBN numbers. It is also a leading provider of bibliographic, statistical, and resource information for publishers, booksellers, and libraries, and one of the few sources that measures self-publishing as an industry. An October 2013 release of US ISBN data showed[3] a 59 percent increase

---

1 "Thinking of Self-Publishing Your Book in 2013? Here's What You Need to Know," Forbes.com, accessed July 5, 2014. www.forbes.com/sites/nickmorgan/2013/01/08/thinking-of-self-publishing-your-book-in-2013- heres-what-you-need-to-know/
2 Bowker, Bowker.com, accessed July 5, 2014. www.bowker.com/en-US/
3 Bowker US ISBN data, Bowker.com, accessed July 5, 2014. www.bowker.com/en-US/aboutus/ press_room/2013/pr_10092013.shtml

in self-published titles between 2011 and 2012 — up 422 percent from 2007. The report also concluded that 40 percent of those 2012 titles were ebooks.

Many factors go into a book's success from a sales and marketing perspective. Here are a few questions you'll need to answer. In the download kit you'll find a worksheet called Writing a Book: Define Your Demographic to help you record your answers:

- Who is your demographic? Everyone is not your target reader. The more you can define who your project is for, the easier you can find out to whom and where to market.

- Once you establish who your target demographic is (e.g., age, occupation, education level, interests), find out where they go for information. Do they prefer video or apps? Are they brick and mortar traditionalists? Maybe they're both. What platform do they prefer for reading?

- What is your purpose for writing this book? Is it about you and your ego, or is it about offering some value or entertainment to the reader?

- Why should the reader care about your story? If there are 1 million books published every year, why should they read yours instead of the 999,999 others?

- Why are you the writer? What qualifies you to write this project? Be able to answer this so you can position yourself differently than the other books written on the same topic.

The two-minute video "We Are the Future"[4] is a must-see. This video isn't just about marketing, it's about publishing. Knowing how someone wants to receive the information is as important as knowing who you want to reach. It doesn't matter if you hate the video or not. If this is your market, it's about what they want, not what you want.

The good news is, what you decide to do doesn't have to be expensive, even if you choose multiple streams of delivery.

Anyone who has ever published a book with a traditional publisher will tell you a publisher is not a lottery ticket. A publisher is a partner that will guide you through its process of publishing.

---

4 "We Are The Future," YouTube.com, accessed July 5, 2014.
   www.youtube.com/watch?v=P81bb0Tzwbo&feature=youtu.be

Before you approach a traditional publisher, you should know the following:

- Never submit an unsolicited manuscript. Definitely, don't submit that unsolicited manuscript in bulk to every publisher under the sun in one email.

- Do go to a publisher's website to see if what you want to write about is in the company's genre. Look at the titles the company has published. Has the same book already been published with that publisher? If so, don't waste your time unless you can convince the managing editors you've taken a different angle on the topic.

- Read the publisher's submission guidelines. If it says no emails and you email your unsolicited manuscript, your communication will be deleted or go straight to the spam folder.

- Craft a one- or two-sheet outline and pitch your idea to the publisher first. The submission guidelines will tell you how to send it. In that pitch, have a succinct marketing plan. Don't expect that a publisher will do all the selling for you. If you can't bother to take your book seriously enough to jump in with both feet to sell it, neither will the publisher.

- Reread the pitch letter and outline repeatedly and proof for errors. You don't pitch a book to a publisher, pretending to be a writer, when you can't proofread your emails or pitch letters. Make those words sing off the page. Spelling and grammatical errors will kill your efforts in one swift keystroke.

If the publisher likes your idea, you'll receive a response in which you'll be asked follow-up questions about your book. Sometimes a publisher will accept a book proposal and spend some time discussing it with you. However, until the contract is in your hands, there is no deal. When it comes time for the publisher to send the actual publishing contract, after days of no communication, you might learn the publisher has changed its mind for some reason. I've experienced this twice. It also happened to me when I worked with an agent.

You don't really need an agent to pitch a publisher, unless it is requested in the submission guidelines. For example, my contracts with Self-Counsel Press came after direct pitches from me.

Make sure you read every word of your book contract. I already had the advantage of a prior relationship, so there were no surprises in this book contract with Self-Counsel Press. There was no advance (and there rarely is with many publishing houses). As long as the contract details didn't make my "Spidey sense" tingle, I agreed to the terms. If there was an advance, I probably would have sought a contract lawyer or agent. Any time you're unsure, with or without an advance, do consult with a legal professional.

If there are things you want to change on a contract, within reason, you have every right to make written adjustments. It is all right for an author and publisher to negotiate a publishing contract.

You'll receive a list of deadlines to adhere to as part of the contract. A publisher has a time line for when the book is slated for release. Respect that. If you see that you can't make a deadline, say something well in advance. The partnership is one based on mutual respect and common sense.

2. The Ebook Revolution

Books had been available in digital format for some time before Amazon launched the first Kindle ebook reader in 2007. They came in the form of a PDF. Most of our desktops and laptops are equipped with Adobe Reader — the software that allows us to view a PDF.

We can create a book in MS Word, Microsoft Publisher, PowerPoint, or any other software program to which its files can be saved into a PDF format. We can even view these files in an ebook reader, although it does not view the same way or include the features that make the e-reader unique.

These PDFs are technically known as eDocs, and you can just as easily sell them on your website as you can a physical book.

Google created Google Print in 2004 when it began digitizing all the books it could get its hands on, including those that were still under copyright protection. Two lawsuits prevailed: One a class-action suit on behalf of authors and the other from five large publishers and the American Publishing Association. At the same time as litigation, Google changed Google Print's name to Google Book Search and several university libraries signed on as participants. By November 2008, Google had scanned 7 million books and then chose to add magazines to the mix. A settlement was finally reached between Google and the publishing industry in March 2012. By then, 20 million books were scanned. The lawsuit between Google and the authors was outstanding at the time this book was written.

2.1 Ebook formats

There are more ebook formats than you might think. The following sections discuss two prominent ones.

2.1a Kindle

Figure 7 is a picture of my personal Amazon Kindle. On the right is the folder of books I've finished reading. You can download hundreds of books into this device, which might weigh less than a hairbrush.

On the left is a page in a book. At the bottom, it shows the percentage read, as opposed to page numbers. You can bookmark a page, access a dictionary, and even highlight a section. Highlights show up in a separate text file inside your Kindle with all of the other text you singled out. Each highlight includes the quotation, the book, author, and page number.

Figure 7

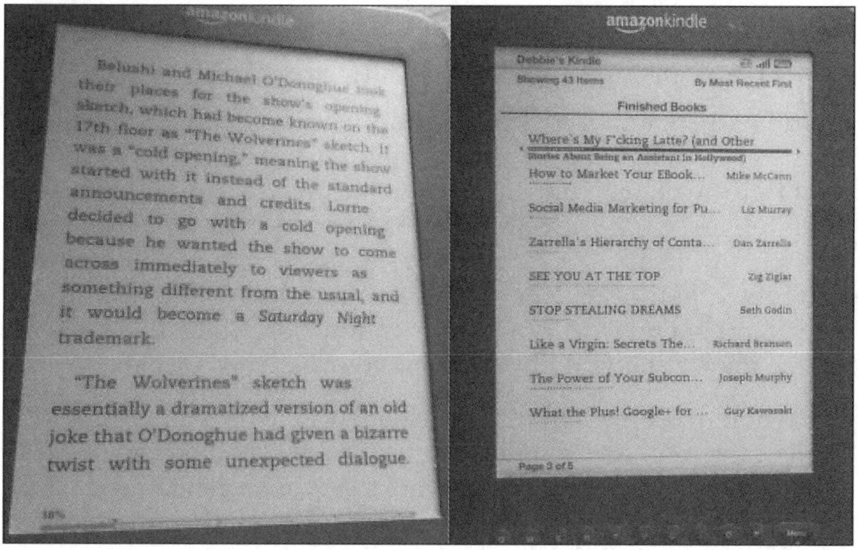

You can plug your Kindle into your desktop or laptop and transfer the folder of book files for backup. Kindle books are also accessible from your Amazon account online. There are Kindle apps for smartphones and tablets, which sync to your account.

One thing makes an e-reader like Kindle so popular is that the device remembers the page where you left off when you shut it down. How many times has the bookmark fallen out of the print book you're reading, forcing you to try and find your place again, only to reread a couple of pages before you realized you already read that information?

It is possible to load a PDF (eDoc) into your Kindle, but you won't have the luxury of the e-reader options, and when you shut down and open it up again, you have to scroll from scratch to find your place.

The electronic file compatible with a Kindle is a Mobipocket, and the file extension reads as .mobi or .prc.

2.1b EPUB

Other tablets offer a similar viewing experience to the Kindle, except on a different screen.

The EPUB (its file extension is called .epub) is for viewing on Apple (iOS) and Android tablets and smartphones, and almost every other device but the Amazon Kindle.

2.2 Ebook conversion and vanity presses

Getting a PDF converted to an ebook format can be a challenge. Print-on-demand (vanity press) companies can do them, but you won't always have control of your files to distribute from your own website. Instead you would insert a link that leads to the developer's website. The print-on-demand company will sell your book itself and offer you a royalty. Note that unlike traditional book publishers, with vanity press publishers you will have to do all the marketing and publicity for your book.

When it comes to print-on-demand companies, do your homework and vet them carefully. Try and connect with a few of their authors to find out what their experiences were like. Writersweekly.com is a great resource. Remember the old saying: If it seems too good to be true, it usually is.

You can go directly to Amazon and get a PDF converted to a .mobi file right on the spot so can sell your ebook through Amazon.

By using Amazon's Kindle Direct Publishing,[5] you keep control of your files and revisions are not a problem. You can also have your book converted into other languages. The bonus is that the service is free!

By the time this book is published, there may be several sites that offer free proper .epub conversions like Amazon does with .mobi. Until then, you might have to do a lot of Google searches to find a freelance designer. Companies that make their money in app building can do the job but the money they receive for a small conversion doesn't come close to what they would get for an app that might bring them thousands. However, it doesn't hurt to ask if you've exhausted other options.

Finding the right freelance artist is hard. So far a lot of graphic designers are still vested in print file development and are not always willing to learn how to do ebook conversions. However, there are some design firms that specialize in ebook conversions.

A word about covers: You can try and craft one yourself in MS Word or MS Publisher and try and marry it to the rest of the PDF, or you can find a professional to do a cover and combine the files for you. Hiring a freelance graphic designer will save you time and grief if you don't know what you're doing. Also, the cover is your selling tool. If it looks terrible, you're ten steps behind the eight-ball!

3. Gamification of Books

Books are about storytelling, and what better way to engage a reader than to get them involved and let them have a say in the outcome. No one has to be a print chauvinist anymore. Books can be fun, engaging, and interactive. Video games are another publishing platform.

A video game is dependent on narratives, drama, and scriptwriting. The participant can have a direct intervention on the plot, so the writing is not straightforward. There is no linear point A to point B. It is described to be more like improvisational theater, so it isn't a big reach to turn a game into a film.

While games have rules, they do not fit into literary form so easily, even though you can create a book as support for a game. You need to see the bigger picture when creating a game. The "reader" has more control and can destroy a plot development by

---

5 Kindle Direct Publishing, Amazon.com, accessed July 5, 2014. https://kdp.amazon.com/

having a character choose a different path. The writer needs many layers and various scenarios in order to flush out the storytelling.

To dive into video game development, do a little research. If you don't play games yourself, find people who do — specifically in the age demographic you want to target. What types of games are they playing, which developers do they like, and why? To learn about the gaming industry, your best bet is never to go to an agency, or even a developer (at least initially). Gamers are like bingo players and comic book collectors. They are the experts. Their knowledge will make your head spin.

If you can't think of a gamer in your family or your circle of influence, go to social networks and put out a request that you want to interview some seasoned avid gamers to get some direction on your project. Believe me, they will know where to steer you and to which developer. You'll learn what is lame and what not to do in a hurry.

While a book can be a game, a game can also be another way to build an interactive story by using another platform.

4. Apps

An app can be static or include various forms of interaction. There is no limit to what you can do in an app. You can let your creativity run wild.

The cost of app building will vary, depending on the degree of creativity. Of course, a static app will be less than a fully interactive one. Apps are built more like websites using code, so the more complicated the code, the more expensive it will be to build.

Sometimes you'll see apps available in both iOS (Apple) and Android; other times an app may be available in only one platform. The owner decides which platform to use first; and later on the app may get built in the other platform — or he or she could launch both at the same time.

The demographics can differ between Apple and Android. If your market is highly educated and well-off, they could steer toward Apple. If your demographic is in the working class, Android might be more popular. However, that isn't a hard and fast rule. Research the statistics for each platform to determine if your audience fits one or both platforms. An app can be built in one platform and then mirrored in the other platform, but the task still requires creating codes and tedious technical work.

Video or audio clips can be embedded into an app. It can also have callout boxes with quick quizzes, links to other websites or social networks, and pop-ups. An app developer can help you be even more creative.

Let's look at a children's health and wellness program for example. This is part of a brainstorming session I had with someone who works in the fitness industry. The app had about six buttons, representing different "pages" or tabs of content. A couple of them included:

- Cyber-creating a recipe in which the user is encouraged to submit a modification.

- Shopping in a viral food store, which teaches children how to look for grocery items for various recipes.

- A game similar to *Operation* that has an interactive game page that features the anatomy of a person, where one can point out and diagnose types of illnesses.

If you were writing an adult nonfiction book, you could build it as an ebook with app features, such as a callout box with embedded audio, where the author adds a 30-second clip to further a point. How about a walkout video[6] with a message from the author or someone else telling a story? There could be a direct link for the reader to personally message the author, or engage with an instant messaging service.

5. Digital Comics

The graphic novel — a novelized comic book — is a highly popular genre. It can cross into digital media in animated form.

There are a few ways to create animation, including anime (Japanese animation) and machinima (animated stories in real-time virtual game format). You could include special features on DVDs and print-on-demand a custom digital comic playlist. Similar to app building, it is only limited by your creativity.

The main elements of a graphic novel are illustrations and storytelling. William Kuskin, a University of Colorado professor,

---

6 "'Walkout' examples for websites," YouTube.com, accessed July 5, 2014. www.youtube.com/watch?v=5-_BlS3iUjg&feature=youtu.be

described the comic in his Comic Books and Graphic Novels course: "Comics stand on the boundary line between art and entertainment. The reader is an accomplice. The reader is a key part of the interpretation."

A comic has multiple entry points into a page (i.e., scheme, form, and arrangement of words). It can be a complicated art form, and yet it is simple at the same time.

If you've never picked up a comic before, that will be your first task before you can create one. Your local public library will have numerous books about comics and it may also have comic books. If you don't have a library card to check out books, just do your research at the library, for free. Outside of that, the Internet has virtually endless resources. Check out free online educational resources like Coursera.org to see if there is a course about comics.

If you are already an avid comic enthusiast, you probably have an idea of publishers you like. Check out their websites to see their submission guidelines.

If you feel you have the resources to create a comic on your own, using your own illustrator and graphic designer, use all the online platforms to get it in front of the world. Look for comic distribution sites and other platforms that are specific to that genre.

6. Photography

A story can be told by photographs, or you can use photographs to support a story. Photographers have a lot more control over distribution now than they did when they relied solely on media and physical galleries.

If you are a photographer, where can you publish your work? There are numerous digital galleries to showcase your wares, such as Flickr, Instagram, Imgur, Pinterest, Picasa Web Albums (Google), ImageShack, and many more.

Submit your work to Wikimedia Commons, where your photograph can be used by anyone who offers you credit. This may help you build a following of your work.

There is a community of photographers on Google+ that you can tap into. They each create a following by sharing their work for free. You'll find some of the most stunning photography you've ever seen shared and re-shared several hundred times.

Virtual Photo Walks has almost 4 million followers on Google+ and has found a way to bring photographs to life. Its tagline is: "Walk the walk for those who can't." Founder John Butterill uses Google+ Hangouts on Air to share photo walks. For example, a veteran who is holed up in a nursing home is able to revisit the beaches of Normandy as a photographer is live on the scene, using his camera to share the video with the rest of the people on the Hangout.

7. Music

The music industry set the tone for the book publishing world years back. It was faced with reinventing itself when the digital download appeared. That meant the indies (independent music producers) were finally able to compete with the studios, which ended up creating a growth in music publishing.

Similar to photographers, musicians have more control over their art than they used to. Nowadays musical artists have a lot more advantages in making themselves known by using the digital tools at their fingertips.

iTunes, Amazon, Spotify, and Pandora are a few of the more sought-after platforms people want to get their music onto. There is no one-size-fits-all in this market just as there isn't in traditional book publishing. Each of these sites has specific instructions as to what you need to do in order to have your music considered.

MySpace is still a popular network for musicians to feature their work, but SoundCloud and ReverbNation are a couple of alternatives or complements to that platform. SoundCloud is a website specifically for music and audio creators to share their work for free. ReverbNation offers a couple of options for selling your music.

The best way to get your music on the major sites such as iTunes is to have a music aggregator. An aggregator is a distributor that supplies music to online digital retailers. Some aggregators charge an up-front setup fee; however, it is likely most artists choose the ones who take a cut of the sale. There are a few things you need to consider, such as song licenses, and public domain material, but one only has to go as far as his or her keyboard to find an answer or two before proceeding. Start your research by going to Graham Way's blog called "Demystifying the Music Biz."[7]

---

7 "Graham Way's Blog," accessed July 5, 2014. http://grahamway.ca/blog/digital-music-distribution-choosing-an-aggregator

8. Film

Netflix is to the television and film industry what Amazon is to books. It has opened the doors for on-demand viewing of not just movies, but popular television shows.

The cable companies still control much of our viewing content, but more and more, the Internet is chipping away at their customer base. People want to watch what they want when they want it, and only the Internet provides that for television and film.

Netflix and on-demand movies killed the video rental market. Hulu, Netflix, and other on-demand television, plus the ability to watch from a wireless television and your laptop, may wipe out the cable business, unless that industry steps up to compete.

We are at the very early stages of where film and television is going, but we can see the direction it is taking; Netflix launched two in-house programs: *Orange is the New Black* and the Emmy-winning series *House of Cards*. We can expect to see more platforms similar to Netflix developing their own programs in the future, and more binge viewing. Amazon has already followed suit with the release of *Alpha House*.[8]

The future of film and television just got serious. The great news for the industry is it means more jobs and content being created outside of the traditional studio system.

9. What Other People Are Doing

Nazim Beltran is the owner of an Italian web agency, Parkmedia.[9] While web design has been his long-time business, he has been developing a solution for an interactive book, which integrates desktop publications and web applications.

"With tablet devices growing at an incredible pace, I don't think websites are going to disappear, but their roles as a main instrument of communication is going to become secondary," he said. Beltran isn't suggesting this platform will apply to just interactive ebooks. It is a utilization that can be used at conferences and in different conditions.

The technology was still unfolding at the time of this writing. Beltran was in conversation with a university about taking their

---

8 "Amazon Has Finally Made Its House of Cards" Slate.com, accessed July 5, 2014. www.slate.com/blogs/browbeat/2014/02/11/amazon_s_new_pilots_transparent_mozart_in_the_jungle_the_after_the_rebels.html
9 Park Media, accessed July 5, 2014. www.parkmedia.it

publications — not to substitute them — but to set up a download-able complement instrument that could be updated with a content management system. You would change the application, upgrade in real time, and load it on whatever distribution channel you want to use, such as the App Store, Kindle, Google Play, and any future devices that become available. This would mean no more backpacks full of books.

"In the case of an educational project, the student not only has the textbook, he has a whole world around the textbook that he can explore without having to close and go look at a website. It's all integrated," Beltran says.

Meanwhile in the Netherlands and Malta, two individuals have been producing multimedia children's books using advanced animations and game-based learning.

Chantal Harvey is the publisher of Netdreamer Publications[10] and Tony Dyson is well known as the creator of the beloved *Star Wars* character R2D2. They have been using *Second Life* as an animation platform to create ebooks. (See Figure 8.)

Figure 8

Source: Clive and the chickens from Bobbekinworld (http://bobbekinworld.com/gallery/

Using machinima, they craft a virtual story with gaming foot-age. This technique pushes the limits of storytelling. Their project

10 Bobbekinword, accessed July 5, 2014. http://bobbekinworld.com/

Bobbekins is 25 snippets of film that can be watched on an iPad with narration. It comes with basic text, music, and graphics.

"I went into *Second Life* and realized it was a great place to make animation," conveys Dyson. "I was also working on the idea of children's books and thought, if the avatars of fantasy creatures in *Second Life* are best when you're filming them, why not go for it? With the animation, you can make stills. Stills can go into a printed book or a Kindle.

"It is easy for anyone to publish, now, and I recommend it for everybody. For making money, one has to be very smart and know where the market is at. You walk into any coffee bar and a child has a tablet in front of them."

Harvey and Dyson did a printed version of *Bobbekins* more for personal reasons: They wanted to have a physical book. "[It] is more of a vanity thing. It would be great if it sells well, but we're not really looking at it from the marketing side," concedes Dyson.

Netdreamer Publications is planning three versions of the book: Kindle, print, and animated, but they plan on putting it into 22 different formats overall.

Dyson is blunt when it comes to marketing. "All the rules are broken. When people say, yea, well I don't really know about marketing. You're in trouble. If you can't do the marketing, don't write the damn book and do self-publishing. Go to a vanity press, get yourself a book, make it look nice, and put it on the side, and say Merry Christmas."

He adds that the big advantage of a publisher is the distribution and that the publisher can put it in a store. In order to get the attention of a publisher, you must understand social marketing. If you can't do that, the publisher won't take you on. The royalty is nothing to write home about, either. He maintains that you'll make no money, so accept the fact you'll be doing workshops and lectures to augment that income.

"So many people want to be in print, which is why vanity press does so well. The aspect of people paying money to create something to show other people is nice. There is nothing wrong with that. It means they sat down and put their heart in it. I have a friend who publishes a book of poetry every year as a Christmas present for his friends and family. That's great because he's actually achieving something and creating something.

"If it's going to be that you want to make money, you want to make a business of it. Then it's going to be writing it and learning about selling it," Dyson says.

Harvey admits when she started out, she didn't really set out to publish books. She was more interested in the digital side. Then she saw that the animations she was creating could be used in a book.

"When we got to that stage with the idea, I got really excited. We had been making machinima. It's real-time animation. We've been doing that in *Second Life* for a while and doing a lot of research. In children's books, I find the animation a bit clumsy. Some of them aren't as good as they could be. To put real CGI [computer generated imagery] in — that's going to make it so expensive. So I think we have a real winner here."

"The biggest problem with our animated book is we can't get them on the biggest platform: Amazon," affirms Dyson.

The platform can't handle it yet, but they are both hopeful it will catch on eventually. They know by using the animated platform that they are limited in the marketplace.

According to Dyson, "We find that people who successfully sell books also sell the idea behind the book. They come up with nice ideas for giving away presents and prizes. They'll give mothers something they can actually use with their child. Really get active with the people you are targeting your book for."

Harvey adds, "Everybody has the dream of writing a book. Evidentially, everybody thinks they're a writer. I used to think that. And you focus on the book and don't focus on all the important things. If you don't learn, and don't study on it, you end up with a really nice book, and then what? Nobody is buying it. You don't know where to put it. If it is not in the store, if it is not available, people can't find it, and nobody will buy it.

"When you start looking into formats, some of them are incredibly inexpensive. In the case of Amazon, it's totally free. It is true you don't always own your content, even on Facebook and sites that are similar. With Amazon, you own the rights but it has the right to extract some of it for marketing."

Dyson and Harvey recommend you get a website, if available, in your name. You're the author. From there, learn Amazon. Then learn the social sites and how they operate. After that, it's up to your imagination.

"Most people, in my opinion, even if they have the money, often spend it wrong," laments Dyson. "They'll spend $30,000 on a course on how to be a self-publisher. The trouble is, they end up not knowing anything. Instead, get a couple of sensible books (when you read them, they make sense to you). Find out who you like, and their style, and learn yourself. Nobody can afford to stand back and let others do it for you, unless you've got the deepest pockets going."

Dyson knows if you get past a certain point of quality, people will take it for granted. They learned that with animation. It gets to where people only notice when it's bad quality. When it's good quality, they expect it. Why not? They're used to Disney. However, good quality means it will cost more to make.

"When I was back making robots, I had another company, besides the special effects studio. It was called Rent-a-Droid. I would take these robots around to big meetings, conferences, and they used to rent them out for a fair amount of money. I made a little robot called TD — looked a little like R2 but it had sort of a skirt around it, more simplified. The amount of people who came up and said they loved it was great. There were others who said, 'Oh, I don't think that's as good as R2D2.' I'd say, 'It didn't cost as much as R2D2.' They would look at it and criticize it and compare it to something that cost a lot of money and a lot of time. It's the same with animation. They're so used to *Star Trek*, which was an absolute bomb to make and a couple of years' time, and they look at our simplified animation and say, 'That's not as good as *Trek*.' No, it's not as good as Trek, but it's pretty good for what we've done. It's good for the price, and it's very entertaining."

People have the ability to write a book and get it published without getting a publisher. There is a feeling that comes with a printed book. It depends on one's age group. If you're into self-publishing, and you're into books, you're probably into printed books.

"I think the platforms are very good together, all of them," proclaims Harvey. "When TV came and everyone said it would kill radio, has it? No. Every new technique just adds to it.

"I resisted computers for a few years, too. Not like Tony, who was an early user. I now think back and ask why? We seem to do that with new techniques and new developments. They probably scare us. Why? I have friends who say, 'Oh, I'm not doing that Facebook or all that weird stuff you're doing.' I don't even defend it anymore."

Dyson foresees that when this generation dies off, the next generation will not be buying the same amount of books. "We know that because the bookshops are closing. Publishers know that because they're not giving it out [profits] to the authors. They're not selling the amount of books they used to. It's the same thing that happened to newspapers. They're not paying reporters any longer. They're actually paying a lot less to bloggers who are writing the articles for them. Some of the bloggers are just happy to be in print. That will continue to happen, until this generation is gone — the people who like holding a newspaper while having their breakfast or while on the train."

The future may not be that difficult to see. The tablet will be where we go for our books.

Publishing comes down to — what is your aim? What is your goal? If you want to make money and make it a business, then you have to be in all the platforms, learn how to do the different formats, learn your demographics, learn your target market, learn how they feel and where their drinking hole is, and learn all their motives. These are the things you have to do.

The problem right now is the platforms haven't caught up to the technology. Harvey and Dyson thought that the Kindle Fire was going to do it for them, but it's still not quite working out. The interaction, which is what they are aiming for, isn't worth spending the time on making it good when there isn't a platform for it. If they can build up their website, then they'll reconsider. By then, maybe Amazon will have caught up.

Considering that the Internet has made the world global, one thing to think about for expanding your project's reach is to have it translated into other languages. While you might have the perfect editor for print, audio, and animation, that person may not be the one you can use for Spanish, Chinese, or any other language conversion. Translating a project doesn't mean it is guaranteed to sell in that language's country. It could be an exceptional market in English, and it may tank in Chinese; or it could sell volumes in Spanish, but English sales are mediocre.

Dyson warns when it comes to translating, "Pay well for it or you might find yourself in trouble like some of these big corporations. You do an app version and then find out they said something very naughty [in the translation]."

No matter what type of book you do or what platform it is in, it all comes down to one thing: marketing. Harvey maintains it is important to be in social media. "There is a quote I was told in art school quite a long time ago: More or less, anybody can make a painting, but it takes a genius to sell it."

It's not what people want to hear, whether they're a writer or an artist. They'll say, "I don't want to get involved in marketing." They don't want to get involved because they don't understand it. There is no option. If you're in publishing, you're involved.

Harvey makes a great point: "If you don't understand it, how can you hire someone who does?" You won't be able to tell if the person you hired is feeding you a line. Your only choice for success is to be a student of marketing.

It isn't as intimidating as you might think. It can be as simple as making someone's day on a social media post. Harvey shared an incident about a little girl who liked the video of the Bobbekins dancing that Harvey and Dyson had put on the Bobbekins' Facebook page. She would dance like them, too. Then someone told Harvey it was the little girl's birthday. Harvey went to the Facebook page and said, "Hello … have a happy birthday. Bobbekins say hi."

The little girl went crazy. She said, "Mom, Mom, the Bobbekins are talking to me." She was dancing all day.

"On Facebook, you can directly say hi to fans and interact," adds Harvey. "That's fabulous. That's social media."

Build a platform, understand how it works, keep people entertained, build your followers, and be personal. Those are the keys to marketing in social media no matter what platform it is built under.

3

Position Yourself

"Own the land where the deer live and stop hunting. Under the radar marketing — your content shows up in front of the right people. Good content is shared. The moment you stop mentioning a product by name is the moment you shift from salesman to advocate."

MICHAEL STELZNER

Are you planning on being a one-shot wonder or do you want to create staying power? Do you believe in your own message enough to do the work and push it out? Treat your book like a business and your message like an empire. If can't do that, here is your bus stop. No transfer required.

It doesn't matter whether you launch a movie, start a website, sell an app, or write a book, winging it is not an effective plan. This isn't to say that you won't have some success if you just dive in. Action is better than wishing, after all.

1. Find Your Target Market and Anticipate Where It Is Going

As mentioned in previous chapters, everyone is *not* your market. It doesn't matter what you sell, position yourself to the right audience. So how do you figure out who is your target market?

There is one surefire way to help steer you in the right direction: Ask people. However, you need to ask the right people. For example, don't ask the 40-year-old advertising executive what a 20-year-old will like. Don't ask a 50-year-old golf pro where to get the best longboards. If you want to know something about a certain demographic, go to that demographic and ask them.

What is your ten-year-old daughter into? What media does she spend all of her time using? It doesn't matter if you like what she is into or not. The child is not about to make a special trip to Walmart to buy a Billie Holiday CD. Instead, she'll be downloading Katy Perry's latest song from iTunes or checking out a One Direction video on YouTube. She may end up asking you, "Dad, what's a CD?" If not now, wait a couple of years.

How many times have you tried to call your teenager on his smartphone? How many times has he answered? Has he ever responded to an email? You probably text him or send him private messages on Facebook. How fast does he respond to that?

How you like to receive information isn't how your audience may want to receive it. This is a world of blended technology, as opposed to being singularly analog or digital. Consider multiple applications to market your message, or to create your product. Always remember that your product is your business — unless you're making it to give to the family for Christmas presents.

Know something about your audience. In many cases, there are multiple age groups, cultures, income brackets, statuses, and more. Break down each variable and learn as much as you can about each — right down to the underwear they wear, if you can. The more you know about the people you are targeting, the more you can find where they are in order to reach them.

Does your target market take the train to work? Transit riders may be looking at tablets, smartphones, and Kindle devices. Do they drive? Drivers may prefer audiobooks.

Niche markets are actually easier to target than general markets. You can fine-tune exactly what that group looks like. Once you figure out where they are, that's where you go to spread the message. You wouldn't advertise beer at an Alcoholics Anonymous meeting any more than you'd post a fan page for a nursing home on Snapchat.

Understand your target market and work at staying ahead of what everyone else is doing. Be in the position that when people are scrambling to catch up with the changes, you are already there.

There are two famous individuals you want to position your business after: Wayne Gretzky and Madonna.

Wayne Gretzky is arguably the best player who ever graced the ice in the National Hockey League. Why was he so successful? He went where he anticipated the puck was going to be, not where it was going. After his playing career, he dabbled in coaching, managing, and maintained his role as one of hockey's greatest ambassadors, but if he goes back to his on-ice philosophy, his next venture will soar.

Madonna did not maintain her success by resting on her laurels. Yes, she used controversy and shock value to get attention — and it worked. However, that only goes so far. What she did do was keep reinventing herself — her image and her music — to fit the times. When she starts having difficulty doing those high kicks and her bras are no longer as perky, I'm sure she will make the lounge singer act very cool. Although, Tina Turner is an example of a person who never slowed the pace of her concerts but rather added more vibrant dancers and other effects to fill in for where she was lacking in dance stamina at age 70! If you don't believe me, check out her video on YouTube![1]

2. Discover Your Selling Feature

What is the feature benefit — the end result — that your audience will acquire from experiencing your product? That is your selling feature, and what you will use to position your message to get people to care. Sell what you deliver, not what you do.

Car ads do this well. In 2008, Cadillac[2] created a CTS campaign using women drivers and put the viewer in the car to "feel" the

---

1 "Typical Male" by Tina Turner, YouTube.com, accessed July 5, 2014. http://youtu.be/74JNoLKMfGQ
2 "Cadillac CTS 2008 Commercial," YouTube.com, accessed July 5, 2014. http://youtu.be/lmgWYG2Br68

experience of the ride. Chrysler created a campaign, using patriotism, with its "Imported from Detroit" tagline.[3] In each case, the company is selling the feeling, not the car. It's *how* you sell to them and how the message resonates. You can't be all things to all people, so you might as well tap into the strongest niche.

3. Plan for Success

You should create a business plan as well as a marketing and publicity plan for every product and venture. Having your vision written down will help you implement your plans, which will go a long way to help you succeed.

In the download kit there are PowerPoint templates for both a business plan and a marketing and publicity plan. Your plans don't have to be 100 pages long and they don't necessarily have to be in PowerPoint. They can be an outline that you can flush out into more detail as you work through your vision.

3.1 Preparing your business plan and marketing and publicity plan

In the business plan, you'll want to assess your financial goals and resource requirements (e.g., technical assets, support, design). Look at your industry as a whole and assess how you fit in. What are some of the risks? What's the best-case scenario and worst-case scenario?

Define your product, its competition, where it fits into the marketplace, how it's packaged, how to fulfill orders, and what your launch strategy will be. What is your initial schedule to get things going?

The terminology and exact makeup of a business plan might vary from real-life examples. The following list is the bottom line of what the business outsiders care about. Business outsiders could be lenders if you need start-up money to put your plan into play.

- **Executive summary:** This is your business plan in a nutshell, but it will include a lot of the key aspects of your plan, including vision, rollout, and part of your business outlook. It should also answer the question (especially if you're looking for financing): What are you looking for? It offers just enough meat to get people to read more.

---

3 "Imported from Detroit," YouTube.com, accessed July 5, 2014. http://youtu.be/SKL254Y_jtc

- **Business concept:** What is your business really about? What makes it unique and what is your vision? This section describes all of those aspects in detail.

- **Background information:** What research have you done on who your competitors are and about the industry itself? This section should include the shortfalls, current status, and future trends of the marketplace.

- **Marketing plan:** Everyone is not your market. You can do a summary overview of how you plan on selling your products and services and then craft a marketing and publicity plan that goes into more details.

- **Business outlook:** What are your business projections? Use some of the elements here that you would see in the management discussion and analysis of an annual report (e.g., history and description of the business, acquisitions, operations, assets, financial position, risks and uncertainties, disclosure, procedures, and policies.

- **Financials:** Here is where you must cut to the chase. It is where investors and bankers will determine if your business plan is worth its salt. What are your financial goals? What is your financial forecast? You can hire an accountant and include a 32-pager that looks like the back end of an annual report, or you can simplify this section and bottom line it in two or three sections. This area is about cash flow, profit and loss forecasts, and what you expect in sales. Add in proven revenues you currently experience. If you are using this business plan to solicit funding, be specific and break down what you will use this money for, line by line.

- **Next steps and long-term goals:** What is your roll-out plan? What will your return on investment look like? What are the social and economic benefits? What do you want to accomplish in three years, five years, and ten years?

- **Team:** Who are the key players that will determine the success of this business? Add in a bio for each that speaks to the person's experience related to the business.

Your marketing and publicity plan will cover what you plan to do to get your product or venture noticed. When you are creating your plan, try to include all aspects surrounding your product's promotion (e.g., public relations, advertising, promotions, pricing, distribution). How will you measure marketing and publicity success? Note that success doesn't always have to be about money. For example, you may receive many retweets on Twitter or your video may go viral. Your marketing and publicity plan should include the following information:

- Marketing mission statement
- Marketing team
- Market summary
- Opportunities
- Target customers
- Competition
- Goals and objectives
- Marketing platforms (e.g., break down the types of platforms you'll use such as website, Facebook, Twitter, Amazon, TV)
- Public relations (e.g., press releases, press conferences)
- Speaking and training

Resource requirements (e.g., design team, web professionals)

- Product and services (e.g., DVDs, MP3s, books, podcasts, t-shirts)
- Revenue projections (i.e., financial aspects of the plan such as how much you'll make from speaking engagements or book sales)
- Launch (i.e., information about the launch platforms, time lines)
- Contact information

4. You Need the Internet More Than the Internet Needs You

You may think you don't need to be on the Internet, and that what you're doing on a face-to-face level is working for you. Whether you're an individual or a business, the Internet is probably where your audience spends most of its time. Your readers could already be talking about you. Will you be there to field the questions?

Erik Qualman[4] is the digital Dale Carnegie of our time. He is a renowned Internet thought-leader, who penned one of the first bibles of social media: *Socialnomics: How Social Media Transforms the Way We Live and Do Business*. He has also written *Digital Leader: 5 Simple Keys to Success and Influence*, and *What Happens in Vegas Stays on YouTube*. His "Social Media Revolution" videos have been the most viewed social media video series worldwide. He has been named a Top 100 Digital Influencer by *Fast Company* magazine.

The Internet offers up a whole new world for marketers, but there are rules. Qualman cautions, "If you don't understand the new rules of reputation, you really are playing Russian roulette with your future. You could think by avoiding these that you could save your reputation. That's not true. It's called a digital shadow. It's what others post about you. Ninety-two percent of children under the age of two have a digital shadow. Whether you're 80 or 20, your reputation is no longer completely in your control."

If you don't post anything and avoid the Internet altogether, then you are allowing others to manage your reputation for you. There will be negative posts, but if we're not proactive in managing our reputation, then that's all that shows up. If we're engaged online, that negative thing may be one small part of the story. Qualman says you don't really want a perfect profile because then it doesn't look like a real person with human flaws.

Create your own online legacy. "The shift today is we don't have to wait for our funeral. Our legacy is in digital ink, permanent ink. Even after we're gone, we can actually have influence over others. You can still contribute through tools." Qualman adds that you have to live your life as if your mother is watching you.

Do an Internet audit on yourself and your business. Look for what people are saying about you in Google under all the tabs (e.g., web, news, images, videos, books, blogs, discussions). Then do a search in social media: Google+, Facebook, Twitter, and see if any conversations or pages come up. This gives you an opportunity to address an issue, and turn your disgruntled customers into disciples.

---

4 Socialnomics, accessed July 5, 2014. www.socialnomics.net

There is a Twitter account, @BPGlobalPR, that is not the official Twitter page of BP Global. This Twitter handle offered some much needed comic relief at the expense of the real BP Global during the Gulf Oil Crisis.[5] The real BP Global site was neither visible during the crisis nor was any member of the BP public relations team. This is a Public Relations 101 example of how a company could have avoided being the butt of the Internet's jokes. Instead of hiding and avoiding public attention, company officials could have stepped up, front and center, and really made a difference in how the oil and gas industry was perceived.

Petroleum is a resource all of us use. Right now, at this moment, everything around and on your person you is either made from a petroleum product and/or was shipped by transportation that required oil and gas products. Water, toothpaste, computers, smartphones, pencils, makeup, hair products, the soles of your shoes, coffee creamer — unless it was grown in your backyard, it is connected in some way to oil and gas. Even then, the seeds you planted and the tools you used to dig the carrots out of the garden all came to your home via an oil and gas product. However, this is not the message that comes from the oil and gas industry. Do you see the opportunity here? No, it won't change anything about the results of the spill, or the fact that people, wildlife, and livelihoods died. But by stepping out and using Twitter and Facebook to engage angry citizens in a respectful fashion, and facing the media — this may have helped BP avoid becoming public enemy number one.

5. Internet Trolls: Cyber Libel and Cyberbullying

Not everyone plays nice on the Internet. Sometimes it can get downright nasty and no one is immune.

Internet security expert Rob Cairns[6] says before anyone should trust a post or website that is dedicated to libeling a person, he or she should check out the subject on Twitter. There you'll be able to see true character in his or her feed.

The ugly post may be the only thing detrimental on the Internet, regardless of where it ranks in Google. As awful as the post may be, the people who know you, know you. They won't believe the post is true.

5 "100 Days of the BP Spill: A Timeline," accessed July 5, 2014. http://content.time.com/time/interactive/0,31813,2006455,00.html
6 Robert Cairns, accessed July 5, 2014. www.robertbcairns.com/

The person who has authored the ugly post has likely broken the law through an act of cyber libel or cyberbullying. That may be a clue about its source. When someone makes such an effort to libel another person that says more about the author of the nasty post than it does about the person he or she is trying to besmirch.

The first action step you need to take is to *not* feed the bully. Do not engage that person under any circumstances. Instead, document and gather evidence. Take screenshots of everything and keep a file. (If you don't have a Print Screen key on your keyboard, Google the keywords: "how do I take a screenshot with … ," then name your device.)

Cyberbullying and cyber libel are against the law. Reclaim your power and go to the police and file a report. Even if the police are unable to prosecute (which could be for any number of reasons, none of which means you don't have a case), get a case number. Document everything. Note that the laws are similar but not exactly the same in the United States[7] and Canada,[8] as well as other countries.

You may not be able to move that post out of sight on Google, but what you can do is take control of your own content and post good stuff to try and drown him or her out.[9] Use common sense when you post, too. Don't become what your cyberbully is, no matter how tempting it may be. Don't respond to the post, because that will engage the author.[10]

When does a website or web post cross the line? If the post has the intent to harm, then it may be breaking the law. One can face serious fines and up to five years in prison (in Canada). Just know if it happens to you, you're not alone.

While the Internet does open up the world of publishing and marketing, it also means people now experience similar trashing that you see with the likes of celebrities. Knowing this should give you pause when you see a nasty post in a Google search that is incongruent with what you know or have heard about a person. The best way to fight back is to create engaging posts of your own.

---

7 "US Internet Law/Defamation," Wikibooks.org, accessed July 5, 2014.
   http://en.wikibooks.org/wiki/US_Internet_Law/Defamation
8 "Canadian defamation law," Wikipedia.org, accessed July 5, 2014.
   http://en.wikipedia.org/wiki/Canadian_defamation_law
9 "Ugly Internet Posts Are Temporary, Sort Of," Internet Billboards, accessed July 5, 2014.
   www.internetbillboards.net/2014/02/09/ugly-internet-posts/
10 "10 Steps to Do When You Discover You've Been Cyberbullied or Cyber-libeled," FreelancePublishing.net, accessed July 5, 2014. www.freelancepublishing.net/wp/2014/04/29/when-you-discover-youve-been-cyberbullied/

6. Content Curation

Content curation is the process of collecting, organizing, and displaying information relevant to a particular topic or an area of interest. Curating can help you establish a following and a place in a community where people go to find information on that topic. Look for the industry thought leaders on a topic and use curation to build relationships with them.

Everybody on the planet has the means to be a publisher, and with so much content being created, getting found can be difficult. Content also has to be more than aggregated material or it becomes a drive-by link.

Tom George is the founder and CEO of Internet Billboards,[11] a content curation website, where thought-leaders post subject-specific topics and timely news.

When you find a great piece of content, George suggests you add your own personal touch to it, a reason why you think it is shareable. "Retitle an article. If I'm an author and took my time to create really good content, by definition, curating a piece should in no way take anything away from the author. The author should feel good about you curating it. The piece you curate, you want to give it some in-depth analysis. Don't just copy and paste. Make it valuable."

In reality, when you see a good link, stop, slow down, highlight a couple of points from the article, and maybe add your own viewpoint. What you add and how much will depend on the platform on which you are sharing it.

George asks, "How much content is being created on a topic? How many new original articles are being published every single day? How are you able to develop the relationships you have within the topic community?"

Develop a content curation plan. Don't just randomly curate things. Figure out what your overall point is for sharing. What are you trying to do? Be strategic. Curation is not a substitution for creation.

"You have to have some thoughts of your own," says George. "You should write some content once in a while. Have a content marketing program in place and editorial of how you're going to publish your content."

---

11 Internet Billboards, accessed July 5, 2014. www.internetbillboards.net/

This may seem like a daunting task. It is true that a lot of businesses have difficulty committing to writing a full article once a week.

If you're just starting out, curation can actually help support your content marketing strategy. One way to do that would be to get on the good curation sites, set up some topics, and write a couple of posts each month. Build your own network using these tools. Good curation sites include Internet Billboards, Scoop.it, and StumbleUpon.

Get to know the curation community and the people that are in it. Ask questions. Stay in touch once or twice a week. Ask people in the community what they want to get from the information posted by other members. Is there something you can do to help?

"If you're going to spend your time consuming the content to learn, then you might as well hear what the other thought leaders have to say and get involved in the content as a community. Content curation is a way to start conversations," George says.

Curation can help build your knowledge base and circle of influence. It's easy to start; however, it is hard to stick with it and build up your followers because it does take time and work to do it well.

4

Finding Monetary Resources and How to Get Paid

Raising money for a project is not easy. It has been said by many that the first million is the hardest to make. That said, whether you need $2,000 or $2 million, the task of raising funds is the same: difficult. Money does not fall out of the sky with the snap of your fingers.

If traditional sources (e.g., bank loan) don't work out for you, friends and family are unable or unwilling to chip in, you can't find a joint venture partner, and potential sponsors are not returning your calls, then knocking on doors and finding alternative sources of funding may be the steps you need to take to get the financing you need for your business.

When it comes to money, checks are becoming an archaic system. Check technology sits right up there with a telex and typewriter, or DOS and Windows Millennium Edition. Unless you request them, many banks don't even offer checks anymore with a new account sign-up. They're just not that into them and they will put holds on them to ensure they don't bounce before depositing. Electronic banking is where it's at. The following sections discuss recommended e-commerce solutions.

1. Crowdfunding

Crowdfunding is a way to get the Internet community to pool resources to support your cause. You propose an idea, product, or project and find people willing to donate and support your work. Of course, nothing is guaranteed, and each crowdfunding website has different rules for reaching a target goal, but overall, there have been many authors and content producers who have successfully raised money to produce their material.

Before you jump in with both feet and get excited about the prospects of having people throw money at you, first check the rules of your country. There are some places where crowdfunding is illegal, and yes, I'm talking about some areas of North America. Different laws in various jurisdictions in some states and provinces may prevent you from using this option. Do your research online or by asking an accountant or attorney for additional information about crowdfunding.[1]

Go to a crowdfunding website (e.g., Indiegogo, Kickstarter) and read about successful campaigns involving similar projects. A lot of time is needed to create a successful campaign. Besides a video, you'll need to come up with cool perk ideas, which is what people get when they actually donate.

1000 Days of Spring[2] is a project that more than exceeded its goal. The following are some of the elements that made this campaign successful:

- A compelling story. A young man hitchhiking around the world on a dime and working odd jobs to continue his journey.

- A good video that captures the essence of the story and the campaign.

- A business plan done well (people want to know what the funds be used for before they will part with their money).

- The purpose behind the campaign.

- Vivid pictures of his travels.

---

1 "Untangling Canada's proposed new crowdfunding laws," Canadian Business, accessed July 5, 2014. www.canadianbusiness.com/companies-and-industries/crowdfunding-securities-regulator-rules-faq/
2 "100 Days of Spring," Indiegogo, accessed July 5, 2014. www.indiegogo.com/projects/1000-days-of-spring

- Regular updates.

- Perks.

Perks represent things that a donor receives for the sake of being a donor. You would offer a certain amount of perks for the price level. The quality of the perk will escalate with the amount of the donation. For example, in 1000 Days of Spring, it started with a $10 donation that netted the donor an ebook. The $30 donation offered a T-shirt and a signed copy of the book. The scale worked its way up to the $2,000 donation, where the author would be a tour leader.

You will need to fully describe the purpose behind your campaign. Consider whether it is for the sake of raising money or a mission — something an investor can sink his or her teeth into.

There are some crowdfunding sites that allow you to keep the donations if you do not reach your target goal, and other sites that have an all or nothing policy. If you don't reach the goal, you don't get any funds.

Once you put the campaign together and launch it that is only the beginning. It is much like creating the project itself; however, raising money is actually harder. Tell people about it and market it. There is an art and science to a successful crowdsourcing campaign. The best advice I can give is to follow the lead of what others did to reach or surpass their campaign goals. Figure 9 is an example of another successful crowdfunding campaign.

2. Electronic Banking

The advantage of electronic banking (for those who are not yet participating) is that there is no hold on deposits and you can get paid faster, whereas a check can be held for up to six banking days. Many banks don't even issue checks anymore with new accounts.

Internet banking is actually safer than ATM (Automated Teller Machine) and in-person banking. This is my favorite way to get paid because it is quick and easy. Banks also consider this their favorite way of making deposits.

Add layers of protection on your own computer by using a Trusteer add-on, to which a link to a download may be supplied by your bank. Trusteer is a free application that adds security to antivirus software and helps to protect confidential data and block online threats from malware and phishing. Once it is installed on your computer, you can set Trusteer to protect you on other websites, such as Google products and Facebook.

Figure 9

3. Merchant Accounts

A merchant account is a way for you to get paid by others who want to use credit or debit cards. Merchant accounts are hardly worth getting unless the volume of deposits warrants it. You also have to qualify through your bank. If your credit rating is less than stellar, look at PayPal as another option (see section **4.**).

No matter how small your operation is, accepting credit card payments is a big deal. Think about it. People use a credit card to pay for almost everything. You could be losing sales by not having this option.

The cost of a merchant account can vary from bank to bank and the amount of transactions or money left in an account can also determine what a business will pay in fees, which include set-up fees, monthly fees, fees per transaction, and cancellation fees. Transaction rates may also be based on the type of credit card a customer uses. Premium cards could net a larger transaction fee charged to the merchant.

4. PayPal

This will be your second favorite way to get paid if you don't have a merchant account for credit cards through a bank. PayPal is easy to use. There are layers of security built in with the site and every payment is vetted before it is put through. It is possible for someone to pay by e-check, but expect a long hold on those payments until the money clears the bank at the payee's end.

PayPal charges a fee per transaction, and it's about 2.5 percent, depending on the size of the deposit. It takes three to five days to transfer PayPal funds into your bank account — and it is done electronically. You can even use your PayPal account to pay for merchandise and services online.

One word of caution: If you receive an email that looks like it has come from PayPal, *never* click on the link. (The same goes for any bank, Twitter, or Facebook email.) Phishers are making their faux emails look more realistic by the hour. If you see a message and you just want to make sure everything is kosher with your account (the emails always try to scare you in thinking something is wrong with it), type in the web address at the top of your browser and go directly to the site from there. Reports have said that a phishing link like these scam PayPal emails is what caused the security breach at Target.[3]

There are many fake PayPal emails floating around the Internet and the company will be the first to tell you to log in directly to its site. Similar to your your bank, if PayPal has a message for you, the company will never email you. You'll see the notification when you log in. Any fake PayPal emails can be forwarded to spoof@paypal.com, to help the company fight some of these Internet trolls.

5. PayLoadz

If you have an ebook, music download, video instructional course, or any other type of electronic content, do your own distribution through PayLoadz. The free account is extremely limited but you can get more services by paying $15 USD a month. If these are

---

3 "Target breach may have started with email phishing," CBSNews.com, accessed July 5, 2014.
   www.cbsnews.com/news/target-breach-may-have-started-with-email-phishing/

your products, it will be money well spent. There may be other similar services, but after using this one for a while, I recommend it highly.

What this service does is it deposits money through PayPal, and once payment clears, PayLoadz immediately distributes the download. You could sell your products on your website with only the PayPal link, but then you have to physically send out the product. This way, PayLoadz sends it out for you automatically.

If you are going to sell more than $15 worth of digital products a month, this is the way to go. Why? Think about your own buying habits. If you pay for a download, you want it right away. You start to think twice about the purchase and its legitimacy if the download isn't sent within minutes. Sometimes we get busy and can't send it out until the next day. This service makes that part of sales a piece of cake.

5
Be Seen and Be Heard

What are you doing now? If it is working, don't stop. Add to it. If it isn't working, listen up: If you think you don't need an Internet profile, think again.

Even exterminators and plumbers get Googled. It is how everyone vets businesses. When you are looking to hire a subcontractor, find a restaurant, or book a flight, what is the first thing you do? You search the Internet. The same goes for your business: If you don't show up when someone searches you, what does that say?

It doesn't matter who you are, if you want people to associate your name with someone knowledgeable in your field and find your work, the Internet is the one place you want to show up. Think of it as a free Yellow Pages ad that is seen in every city and town across the globe.

The invention of the smartphone has all but shoveled the dirt in the printed Yellow Pages' grave. You can look up someone in the online version faster than it takes to bring the book out of the closet.

You have to show up. If you can't be found, you are not on the radar. There are plenty of other businesses that will rise to the top of the feed. Researchers take the path of least resistance when searching for someone to hire.

1. Plant Seeds

There is one way to increase your online profile: Be everywhere, and especially be where your niche market is. The following are the first basics of building a strong online profile, for which we'll go into more detail in the following chapters.

To begin, you will need to have a website. Everything you do should point back to your website. This means adding your website and blog address to your email signature, to your business cards, to your profiles on every website and social network with which you have an account, and even to your book's back cover author bio.

Find every free online business directory you can and post a detailed profile, especially to local ones, even though businesses are no longer local when they appear on the Web. Someone in Finland can just as easily place an order as someone from your own city.

Join a relevant discussion board where your input might be valued. For example, if you find a discussion board that talks about antivirus programs, or maybe a challenge with a specific piece of software, you can add your two cents to that conversation with some valuable information (only do this in areas in which you have experienced something similar to the person asking for help). This is part of the seed planting. Don't flog your website or your product; instead, just answer the question. Your profile will have your contact information if someone thinks your answers are valuable enough and wants to connect with you outside of the forum.

You could also put up a free online classified advertisement for your services or products on sites such as Craigslist or Kijiji.

Create your own blog and offer to be a guest blogger on another site. Some people use blogging as a main tool of engagement and it gives them business leads. Learn from the best[1] and most popular blogs, and integrate some of their ideas with your own.

Write online articles on free article sites, such as EzineArticles and ArticlesBase. If you write unique content for each post, that

1 "The world's 50 most powerful blogs," The Guardian .com, accessed July 5, 2014. www.theguardian.com/technology/2008/mar/09/blogs

offers more value to the cyber community, and ultimately, your search engine optimization.

Set up Google and Gmail accounts. When you set up your Gmail account, set up a Google+ account, include as much information as you can into the "about" section, and especially include a photograph of yourself. (See Figure 10.) Don't hide behind an avatar. Most people would rather connect with someone who appears to be a real person. An avatar gives them the impression you're trying to hide something.

Figure 10

Remember Bill Gates once said he had a vision where every household would have a personal computer? How about those on mobile? According to a 2013 Pew Research Internet Project, 34 percent of American adults own a tablet. Business Insider[2] adds that 1 in every 5 people worldwide owns a smartphone and 1 in 17 own a tablet. These are not numbers that will decrease anytime soon. Be where people can find you without making them use a lot of effort to find you.

Take social media classes and research the best places you should be. Put yourself out there. Talk to people in all the platforms.

Chapter 1 mentioned Aliya Leigh, the digital media producer, author and blogger. Leigh says another way to get found is to share other people's work. "It's karma. What comes around, goes around. People will begin to follow you. If you care and try to help each other out, that will help you."

2 "One In Every 5 People In The World Own A Smartphone, One in Every 17 Own a Tablet," BusinessInsider.com, accessed July 5, 2014. www.businessinsider.com/smartphone-and-tablet-penetration-2013-10

Namechk.com is a website where you can go to see if your name is available in social platforms. Leigh suggests registering your brand name with all those sites, and then you're ready to interconnect. It may take you two days to get registered with all the social media websites; however, once you are signed up, you can buy tools to update your posts. Some of the social sites can be intertwined. For example, one platform might also allow you to simultaneously post the same link in two or three other platforms.

"Do a blog," Leigh advises. "Do a book trailer." You never know where it will take you. "True story. I wanted more followers to go to my blog. I do a lot of film and decided to do a trailer with anime on *Shadow Creatures*. It got the attention of Random House, who invited me to see their offices. They have all the first editions in the lobby — every first edition from the 1800s to now. Unfortunately I wasn't able to take pictures, but it was amazing."

Leigh declares that book trailers are important because people like visuals. A movie trailer gets people interested in watching a movie. A book trailer gets people interested in reading a book, a blog, or listening to a podcast.

6
Create a Website

If you're building a new website today, you are going to spend a lot of time and creativity in coming up with a name, and it might not be a name that completely matches your business. The longer you wait, the harder it is to find a domain name.

Tony Dyson cautions that having a website doesn't mean people are going to flock to your business. You have to decide what you want your website to accomplish. "Do you want it to be a brochure? Do you want to send people there with a credit card? Or do you want it to actually get the search engines to pick up people who are interested in your subject with keywords. If it's the latter, you really better learn what to do, and it can take a lot of your time."

Researching what other websites have done will help you be creative with your own site. Those sites don't have to be in the same field of business as you. There may not be one site that incorporates every element that appeals to you. Pick and choose from different locations. Take a screenshot of the specific elements. Take note of the sites you like the navigation of and how the pages are laid out. When you have an idea of what you want, you can either hire someone to help you build your website or you can find a template online and build it by yourself.

1. Map Your Website

Create a website map. It's a great tool to work through how you want your pages to look. The navigation will be individual to every website, but for an example, it could break down as follows:

- **Home page:** This page might include your blog, quick links (i.e., where you want to lead people such as a newsletter sign-up), most recent press item, and mission statement.

- **Tertiary search:** This is the navigation you see at the bottom of a page which will include buttons for the home page (give viewers a chance to go back to it from any page), contact information, site map (links to every page of the website from one screen), and legal policy (covering your butt if your viewer thinks you can predict the future and you got it wrong).

- **Main landing page:** This is the main topic page. A landing page is any page on which a visitor will "land" when coming to your site from anywhere else.

- **First level navigation:** A secondary page you click through to from the landing page.

- **Second level navigation:** A secondary page you click through to from the first level navigation page.

- **Third level navigation:** A secondary page you click through to from the second level navigation page.

Figure 11 gives you a visual of these bullets to help you map your own website. A blank template is included in the download kit for your use.

2. Balance All the Elements of Your Website

Look at balancing the technical elements, design, navigation, layout, and incorporating search engine optimization tools. The aesthetics and construction of a site includes design and navigation. You have eight seconds when someone lands on your website to convince the person to stay and look around. If the site is difficult to navigate, the viewer will move on to the next company that delivers the same service with a better website.

Figure 11

Website Map for Publisher Name						
ABOUT (LP)	GENRES (LP)	BREAKDOWN OF TITLES (LP)	PRESS KIT (LP)	WHAT'S NEW (LP)	SUBMISSION GUIDELINES (LP)	CONTACT (LP)
>About >Vision, Mission, Values & Goals >General Policies & Procedures >>Content Policies & Prodedures (for author)	>What We Publish	>Book Covers >>Author, Publication Date, & Overview >>>Purchasing Information	>Backgrounder >Media (appearance) >Photographs >Videos	>What's New > In the Queue (Future projects)	>How to Send in a Manuscript	
Legend: LP – Landing Page >First Level Navitation >>Second Level Navigation >>>Third Level Navigation						

So what if Flash is pretty and your web guy can make it snazzy and cool? Flash is evil. It makes a site slow-loading and can be highly difficult to navigate. It also doesn't work on mobile devices. Few viewers want to be held hostage by an eight-second or longer Flash intro. It can be integrated into other website elements, such as an interactive map or image, but a site that is fully built in Flash is more for the agencies who think it is still relevant.

Use visual cues, such as clickable images for category titles, to help visitors navigate and find information quickly. Figure 12 is a landing page that shows images (also known as "buckets") which allow the visitor to click through to specific events.

Ensure the main navigation, such as a horizontal navigation bar along the top of the page, is easily accessible and clear as to what can be found under each category. Figure 13 shows a website where when you mouse over the category in the horizontal navigation bar, the menu drops down to reveal what the second level navigation pages are.

Figure 12

Figure 13

The top right corner is a common location for a global search function and contact information. People tend to read a website in a "Z" pattern so make your landing page fit for important information.

Each click from the landing page — to the second and third level pages — needs to offer more information. Don't waste your visitors' time; each click should bring more meaningful material. The following tips will help make your website enticing to readers:

- Scrolling pages are common. We have a scrolling mouse and we are used to it in the social media and blog sites so there is no need to add a directional arrow.

- Use more white space. It is aesthetically appealing and helps the site look clean and tidy. It lets you focus on the content, reduce the clutter, and add professionalism.

- Use an uncomplicated and reasonably sized font. Acceptable universal font families include Arial, Verdana, and Tahoma. A bad font makes text difficult to read. The ideal font size is nine to ten points. If the business caters to an older population, the font should be larger. Be wary of using black as a background with white font because it makes text hard to read. The ideal font color is black or very dark grey (charcoal) for body text. Make sure the font to background contrast is such that the visitor doesn't have to squint or adjust the zoom on the page.

- Discourage people from leaving your site by including links that open in a new window as opposed to links that leave your site and go to a new site.

- Create clear and concise content with key information at the top.

- Write catchy headlines and make your content speak to the questions you want to answer for the visitors.

Before your website goes live, it needs to be tested and viewed for look and functionality in different browsers, particularly in Google Chrome and Firefox:

- Click and cross-reference every link on every page.

- Test screen resolutions in each browser.

- Test for broken and redundant links, images that don't load, and broken pages.

- Look for spelling errors in the metadata (i.e., descriptions of images and other information) and meta tags (i.e., descriptions and keywords used to describe a page's contents).

The home page layout needs to show what the business is about. The home page can be a blog, but your widgets should describe enough that people will know they came to the right place. Don't make your visitors have to work to get information or they will move to the next site. Landing pages should draw the visitors deeper into the website. A content page may be all that is needed for a potential customer to make a decision.

Keep your website content fresh and regularly updated. If you don't have a game plan to engage people in your website daily (e.g., a question or picture of the day), then every six months, do an inventory of your site to see if the content information is still relevant.

3. Measure How Well Your Website Is Doing

Conversion-marketing goals help you measure email and online inquiries, white paper downloads, e-newsletter sign-ups, direct leads, direct sales, and more.

Use reporting tools (e.g., Google Analytics) to look for shortfalls (i.e., conversion failures) and strengthen areas that are weak. Check for the visit quality. Where are they going after visiting the initial landing page?

Good keywords, meta tags, and meta descriptions will help your site show up in Google and may bring you more visitors. I am no expert on the technological or SEO (search engine optimization) elements of a website, and if you are not either, you can find a site that makes it easy to navigate and build your own (after a little effort of trying to figure it out) or simply hire someone. There are a lot of website snakes out there, so make sure you vet the web person online and through some of his or her clients.

Sadly, the website snakes are a common story. What they do is hold your website hostage from you. They won't give you the login details so you can make your own changes, and you can't get them to make changes. When it comes time to switch host providers, they will make up a story that you owe them money before they will release the information. If you don't have control of your website, you don't have control of your business.

HubSpot's Marketing Grader[1] grades how well your website is showing up in cyberspace. It also breaks down each area and explains how to fix it. Use the website evaluation tools as a guide, not as gospel.

When thinking of keywords and tags, know how you want to be found on an Internet search. For instance, if your business is book publishing, these are some key phrases you can consider:

- Getting a book published.
- Book publishing process.
- Find a book publisher.
- Publish your book.
- Writing and publishing a book.
- Writing a book.
- Ebooks.
- Digital publishing.
- Manuscripts.
- Editing.

4. Should You Create Your Own Website or Hire Someone?

Creating websites isn't what it used to be. A simple website is so much easier now to create yourself with ready-made tools provided by sites such as Network Solutions and HostGator. These sites also provide customer support.

If your website requires a back office (for e-commerce) and more than 20 pages, consider hiring a professional. A back office/end is the part of a website that is hidden from the public Internet. Members or employees of a firm have individual user logins to get in. Once inside, they might be able to see their personal sales

---

1 Hub Spot's Marketing Grader, accessed July 5, 2014. https://marketing.grader.com/

reports, download corporate forms, transfer commissions, and access other tools.

If you don't have the money to pay for a domain name or hosting, consider Wix.[2] You can build a professional looking website free of charge with free hosting. Your domain will include wix.com in the address but it will tide you over until you can upgrade to a paid account. You can also connect your free Wix website hosting to a paid domain name that was purchased through another company for a small monthly fee.

Having a website that is easy for visitors to navigate, is aesthetically pleasing, and offers clear and precise information is the minimal requirement. If you can't do that, you should probably hire someone who can. Remember, the first place people research a business is online, so make sure your website is done well.

<hr>

2 Wix, accessed July 5, 2014. www.wix.com

7
Blogging

"Write something interesting to the people you want to attract, even if it is something you are not interested in."

MICHAEL STELZNER

Author Rael Kalley knows how to write a good blog, but if you ask him why it's been successful, he'll tell you he has no idea. Train Your Brain the RaelWay[1] has touched a chord with readers perhaps because they can see themselves in his posts. He makes it personal — about him, and the people he tells a story about, but it also ends up being a story about the reader. As you know, everyone likes a good story, especially if it makes them feel good.

Use a blog to position yourself as an expert, to share information about a topic, or to cull like-minded followers in a specific genre. When creating your overall brand and marketing your blog, carefully consider how you want to be portrayed. Do you want to be

---

1 "Rael Kelly's Blog," accessed July 5, 2014. http://raelkalley.WordPress.com/

taken seriously as a writer or as an industry professional? Or do you want your blog to be a valuable source of interesting information?

You can have more than one blog. They may be related in content or geared to completely different interests. If you do have more than one interest and they don't tie together, have a blog for each of them. When I was in the thick of sports writing, I had a blog set up for sports information and a separate one for publishing information. A person who wants information about book publishing might not be interested on a report about the National Hockey League.

For each blog post, you need to share it forward to all your social media networks; otherwise, it's just sitting there on the site waiting for people to find it.

1. Blog Well and Blog Often

The more you blog, the more you get noticed. However, if your blog is terrible, and it is clear you spent no time editing your posts for grammar, punctuation, and clarity, you might as well let it die a slow death. Literacy does count on the Internet.

Outline what you plan on writing about and who your target audience is. If you're writing about motorcycle maintenance, you may have a few mothers who own motorcycles, but for the most part, you likely won't be targeting moms with two year olds. Figure out what your unique body of knowledge is, and who you are writing for and sharing it with. Having all those answers before you start is going to give your blog its unique focus. You may not have to fully define an exact niche. If you can identify in your head who you might be writing for, that may be good enough to get started. This is where your marketing and publicity plan from Chapter 3 comes in handy to help you make your vision a reality.

Plagiarism and copyright issues do exist online. If you are going to borrow from someone, either get that person's permission or make sure when you link to the material you include the source. Images are also considered copyrighted material. Anything on the Web is under copyright protection. Having permission is one thing, but you have to point out that this content came from another photographer, writer, or source and that it didn't come from you. If you don't say that, then it looks like it came from you. That is theft of copyright. There is a feature on Blogger and other blog sites in which you can take the link to a picture image and embed the image in your blog. That way the source of the image is automatic, and it adds another searchable element to your blog.

It's important to be consistent with your blog posts, such as setting a time and day each week when you will post — even once a month is an improvement from many other bloggers. As was mentioned in Chapter 1, IISuperwomanII and Marc Guberti schedule their posts to appear at the same time every week. Readers have come to expect this. Being consistent can help you build an audience like these two have.

Optimize your blog's potential for collecting subscribers. Set it up with RSS (Real Simple Syndication) and NetworkedBlogs (Facebook). Also add a subscribe button. These will all keep your members informed when there is a new post.

Your blog needs to be easy to read and eye-catching. Authors tend to be very text-based for the most part. Imagery is important to support the story you want to tell. To make your blog more interactive, you can include video, audio, and links. The more you know about your audience, the more inclusive your blog can be. Some like to read while others like to look at pictures or watch videos. For the video, you can use your own or take a video and embed it from YouTube. Note that the video needs to be relevant and support what you're writing about. The most successful blogs are good at finding a balance of structure in their posts so they reach all of their audience.

As you build your following and circle of acquaintances, you may want to invite some of these people to be guest bloggers. If you can assess another writer has a similar philosophy and can add well researched and valuable content, it can take the pressure off you having to write every post. Don't allow anyone to guest blog. Make sure you vet them carefully.

Through one of my blogs, I found a woman who was a great resource and offered a viewpoint that complemented the rest of my blog. I asked her directly if she would be interested in submitting something. She didn't have a blog of her own and she accepted.

On another occasion, I received an email from someone inquiring about the possibility of guest blogging. That person sent me three links of samples; two of them were the same entry, and the third link was broken. The entry was well written, but the fact she wanted me to include a link to an essay mill made me highly suspect. Essay mills are big business, where students can pay other people to write their essay papers so they can pass university. I challenged her and after another couple emails, it turned out to be a spammer. Initially, she looked like she could have been legit. So the moral is to vet carefully.

The big question when it comes to comments is: Do I turn the comment section on or off? Sadly, there is so much spam that shows up in WordPress blog comments, it's ridiculous. However, if you don't turn on the comments, you could be missing that one person who could change your future. What you want to do is adjust the settings so you have to physically approve every comment before it appears.

Don't forget to add topic tags. This helps people find you by the subject of the blog entry. Topic tags are really keywords. If you just wrote a piece about the Boston Bruins winning game six of the National Hockey League Conference Final against the Montreal Canadiens, here's what your topic tags might be: Boston Bruins, Bruins, NHL, National Hockey League, NHL Conference Final 2014, Montreal Canadiens, Habs, Bruins beat Habs 2014 Conference Final, hockey, ice hockey. You get the picture.

Just like on a website, always make sure the links open in a new tab and keep people physically on your site.

2. Track Your Blog's Statistics

Google Analytics will help you track your blog's statistics. If you are using Blogger, the analytics are right there and show everything including the browser used, how the blog was found, where the viewer came from, and even the device it was viewed on (see Figure 14).

If you can see where your readers are from, but you are targeting different readers, then you will need to revisit your editorial plan and reposition your content to attract the right viewers. If you know that people are finding you from the embedded images more than your tags, you might want to embed more images. If you see certain posts have a much greater reach over the rest, position your editorial to talk more about those topics.

Figure 14

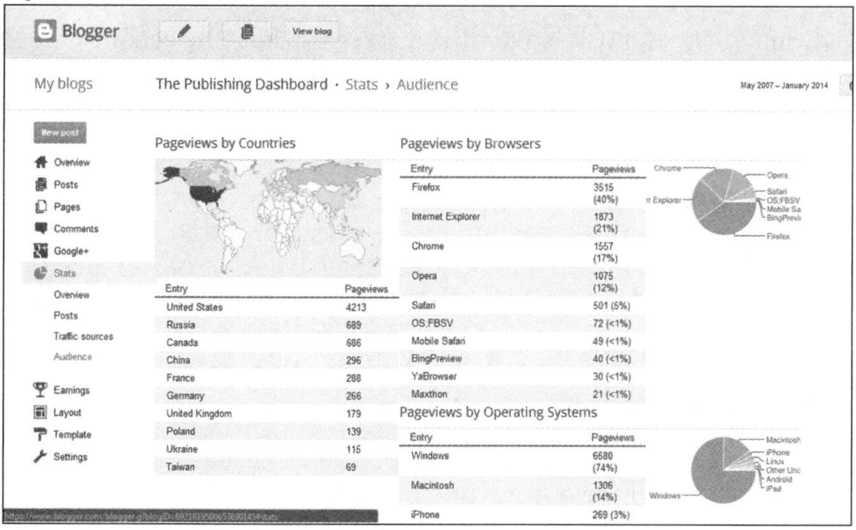

3. What Other Bloggers Are Doing

See what other bloggers are doing and find a happy medium of ideas that work for you. Here are some examples:

- Jeremy Jones[2] uses his blog to generate referrals and clients. He will feature people on his blog, and get featured himself on other blogs. His site is about providing a service to his readers — to help them navigate through social media tools with ease by providing great tips and ideas. Jones is great at commenting on other people's posts as well.

- Chris Brogan[3] shares his experiences, emotions, advice, and offers up a little entertainment in the process. His posts are raw and human, which draws a following.

- Cynthia K. Seymour[4] is Blogger 2.0. She is a go-to resource for all things blogging. One of her strengths is coming up with blog topics, especially when you want to zero in on an issue. She helped me when I was assessing how to deal with a cyberbully by turning a toxic post into a teaching moment, in which I could respond with a positive plan to empower others.

---

2 Ask Jeremy Jones, accessed July 5, 2014. http://askjeremyjones.com/
3 Chris Brogan, accessed July 5, 2014. www.chrisbrogan.com
4 Seymour Results, accessed July 5, 2014. http://seymourresults.com/

3.1 Advice from an avid blogger

Cynthia K. Seymour is an avid WordPress user. She recommends WordPress.org for setting up a blog. What she has to say is good for newbie bloggers but it is an important reminder for seasoned writers, too.

"The first thing you're going to want to do is get hosting. It's about $10 a month. I personally use HostGator and send all my clients there and have them host themselves. A lot of web designers will offer to host for you, but then you don't own your own content. I have my clients host themselves so they aren't shackled to me. They can then come to me because they enjoy what I have to offer," Seymour says.

Seymour suggests signing up for the most basic and simplified package if you're a first-time blogger. Once you sign up, go to WordPress.org and develop an account. Look at blog styles that you like and pick a theme (the overall design). You're going to install WordPress onto your hosting, and then you install a theme.

"A lot of people will get the theme they like raw out of the box, and they don't know how to put it together. If you end up in that situation, you have one of two choices: You can spend two to six months figuring it out or you can hire a WordPress developer to help you."

Having a blog as your primary site gives you a place to post information, your thoughts, your writings, and you actually own your own content. Seymour says that is critical for a writer.

Posting on a social network or another third-party site means you no longer own your content because it is the third-party site owner's content. Also with that content being shareable and being out in the public realm, you have no rights as to where it ends up. This is all spelled out in the third-party site's terms of service.

To clarify what Seymour means is that anyone can copy and paste the content you put on a social network or other third-party site into a document and put it into another platform without you having any repercussions (unless they pass it off as their own material and don't credit you for it, in which case that would be copyright infringement). The sites you post on could shut down tomorrow and you will have lost everything. Your posts would be gone with the service.

In WordPress.com (a free blog site), the terms of service very clearly state, the information is yours and meant for commercial intent. If you have any commercial intent and have your stuff on a free host platform, you are actually violating the host's terms of service. Once you violate its terms of service, it is no longer your information. It's the hosts. The price is you gave it out for free.

There are two levels of WordPress, according to Seymour, "WordPress.org is for people who want to self-host and own their own publishing platform versus WordPress.com is more like a diary. Within WordPress.com, you don't have to pay for hosting. It's completely free, but it's like any of the other social media platforms. That's no longer your content. When you are self-hosting and you own your own space, then you distribute out to the social media networks. People can come back to you in that blog."

If you have any commercial intent about building out, Seymour strongly urges you to self-host. If something happens to your site, your hoster will always have a backup and can usually restore it to the past 24 hours.

The next step is to define your voice and what your subject matter is going to be about. "I have two separate blogs and am about to start a third because I have separate voices. I have Seymour Results, which is more about social media and online content. Flamingo Lips is geared towards Florida and fun things to do. They are two very different voices. Even though I'm one person, it doesn't make any sense to have a blog that puts the two together. They are two different types of conversations."

For most people, if they have too much information coming at them on the Internet, it's intimidating. Respect your reader's time. "If you're going to write 1,000, 1,500 to 1,800 words, that's fine," adds Seymour, "but separate your blog post into different parts. You might also write two to three blog posts instead of the one really long-winded one. You're going to lose people's attention if you don't."

When you lose people's attention with a really long blog post, they don't stay on your page very long. When Google sees that people are leaving too quickly, they downgrade what you're doing. You can be like Internet blogger, Seth Godin, and have a varied style for how you write your posts. Google looks for 300 to 500 words mostly. Every now and then if it's just two to three paragraphs, that's okay.

"You could think of your blog posts as each being a page or each being a couple of paragraphs, as opposed to each being a chapter. You can ratchet each post into a page-sized bite and allow them [viewers] to click onto the next thing or third thing and continue through a series of pages. You could create a chapter of blog posts."

Before we get lost in the lingo, let's define the difference between a post and a page within the context of blogging. Pages are actually shown by the tabs at the top of the website. Posts refer to each individual blog entry.

"Plan out when you're building a blog. The pages could be almost like separate chapters, too. The home landing page might have the most recent posts; a contact page could include links to other networks where you appear; and an about page describes yourself. You might have an archive, a way for people to find out more information. How you structure the blog design is also important for how people will navigate through your space."

Seymour suggests that with every blog post, there is an image. "The best way to get images is to take the picture yourself, even if it's not perfect. The second best way is to purchase an image from a stock image company. But you don't want all of your images to look like stock images or cheesy bubble figures. Then they start to make your posts look dated and not really thoughtful or authentic.

"Be careful about putting in too many stock images. In business, we've seen *ad nauseam* those images of every color person dressed perfectly shaking hands at a business meeting. If you're going to use stock images, use ones that are more unique and not so overused."

Connect and create relationships with other artists, creators, or photographers. Ask them if you can feature their photography or whatever they're doing in your blog. What that does is create a relationship of cross promotion. Make sure you credit them accurately; otherwise, you will be infringing on their copyright. You're also celebrating that partnership or co-creation together. Remember, it's *their* work that is supporting what your words are saying.

"Be ethical and cite your source. If you go to someone else's website, link straight to their website. Don't credit them in name only, but credit them with a URL that would enable a reader to go see their site and drive traffic to them. That way, you are serving both interests. If anyone comes back to you, the thing to do is simply defer, and say 'I'm sorry.' Or ask for permission. It is easy to reach out to people through their blogs, write them a note — 'I would like to credit your image source and use it. Would that be okay with you?' They love it. You've created a relationship with them. You're not just lifting or stealing their work. If they say no, you have to honor that straight up. The absolute no-no is to steal somebody else's work and try to take credit for it. People do that unwittingly, too. I've probably been guilty of it in my past. I'm just much more open and aware about it now."

Seymour starts off her own blog posts with an image, then the supporting text, and a video at the bottom. "Let's say you're writing a blog post on a how-to and you haven't made the video. Someone you look up to has made the video. Include your image, write your blog post, and at the bottom, say, 'If you'd like to learn more about how to ... , here's a great YouTube video called ... .' Name the YouTube video the same name they did. Link to it, and embed the video straight into your post. Then the readers coming to your blog not only have the opportunity to look at the picture, read what you have to write, link to other sources that you've credited, but can also watch a video that might further augment their learning."

Develop a strategy on how you're going to get the blog post out to the masses. "I see a lot of bloggers post something from their perspective that isn't alluring on the other side [from the reader's perspective]. Put yourself in the shoes of the readers. Attract them by submitting your post in such a way that it might draw them in from their point of view. That's where I see bloggers making their biggest mistakes. Always be turning the mirror around on yourself. How would you like to read what you posted if you were on the other side?"

Bloggers may wonder why they're not drawing the traffic they should be. They may not be creating a conversation. They're telling people something instead of creating the conversation that pulls readers in, or asks them a question, or addresses their needs.

Seymour comments, "Put your personality into it, but I think you should be doing that as a writer anyway. It is your voice. I see people trying too hard to push it out and not really identifying what's going to be of interest to the reader."

8
Audio and Podcasts

Nowadays you can create your own radio show for free. The options are endless. You can produce downloadable audio educational files — even audiobooks. As long as you have a digital recorder or a recording feature on your computer or mobile device, you can be a podcaster. The tools are within your device already, or are relatively inexpensive to purchase.

1. Planning a Show and Interviewing Guests

It isn't always easy to line up guests, due to conflicting schedules. The guests have to see the value in coming on your show. Draft a plan for the show to help you answer some key points:

- Who is your audience?

- What is the theme of the show?

- What is the takeaway for the listeners?

Frank Angelone is the founder of SocialTechZone.com; he blogs about social media strategies and tech tips. He also created

STZ Podcast[1] and interviews well-known individuals who use social media and new technologies to improve their businesses.

It first began as a website and blog until he opted to interview someone to add some depth to the site and help it grow. He wanted to associate himself with someone well known. Angelone says, "At the time I did that interview, it wasn't a podcast. I just wanted to interview somebody. After I interviewed Gary Vaynerchuk, I realized I liked this — let me try it again. I reached out to Robert Scoble and was actually shocked that he said yes. After having two pretty big names on, it wasn't even a show yet, I thought, let's see if I can get more people. It escalated from just interviews to an actual podcast."

Angelone does the show more for other people than himself. He wants to hear their stories, what they would do, how they began from nothing, and how they grew their audiences into something.

Because a podcast is less restrictive than radio, he found a schedule that worked for him. He also didn't want to copy what someone else was doing.

"Just because someone has been successful at one idea doesn't mean it's going to work for you. At first I had no idea what I was doing. I was terrible at interviewing. It was very uncomfortable for me. I did it to get over that hump. The more you do it, the more comfortable you feel. When I was starting off with it, I wrote down my questions for each guest. I researched them and tried to find out anything I could about them so I was prepared."

He learns what topic the potential guests have expertise in and what they are most comfortable talking about with him. His research helps him ask the right questions, and then he lets the guests do most of the talking. Angelone tries to be an outsider and not give his opinion. He'll only say something to trigger their opinion. Angelone states that anyone can do this. He's just a regular guy who has developed a simple following.

Booking interviews isn't always easy. When I was a reporter in the National Hockey League, pre- or post-game, I'd have a list of who I wanted to interview, but many times, that player was not available, so I'd go down the list to choices B, C, D, or E. It's no different when you're booking a show. Find someone who fits your editorial guidelines. Have a good outline of your show when you contact them.

---

1 STZ podcast, accessed July 5, 2014. www.socialtechzone.com/wordpress/stz-podcast/lori-ruff-linkedin

Tell the potential guests the following:

- Who you are.

- What the show is about.

- Why you want them as guests.

- What you'd like to discuss.

- Give them an idea of the types of questions you will ask.

- Supply any special instructions (e.g., login, telephone number).

Make sure you research something about your guests. Look at their websites. Check their social media pages. What are their blogs about? Have they been nominated for any awards?

It's up to you if you feel confident enough to roll with the interview without a list of questions. If you do prepare questions to ask, listen to the answers you are given during the interview. Sometimes, the topic might move in a direction where you don't have to ask some of the questions on your list. The conversation might spurn new questions. Go with the flow of the interview.

To learn the skill of interviewing, study those who do it well. When Barbara Walters anchored 20/20, I used to watch her interviews with a pen and paper and jot down her questions. I adapted many of her questions to the one-on-one interviews I had with NHL players.

2. Pay Attention to Sound

Free tools for creating a radio show or podcast don't mean you can ignore your voice or the sound quality of your recording devices.

2.1 Practice your voice delivery

Years ago, during the days when women were not hired for sports teams, other than in the secretary role, I decided that the best way to get more than my toe into the National Hockey League was to become a broadcaster.

CHIT Broadcasting School was owned and operated by a man who became my first mentor: Mel Stevenson. Before I even knew I wanted to sign up, I met with Mel to learn more about this institution. The school was set up like an actual radio station, with a studio booth for the disc jockey and the news and sports announcers to broadcast. Outside of the booth were several desks, a broadcast news teletype, and around the corner was Mel's office. Outside the room, the next door in the hallway was a boardroom. After a brief tour of the main room, this is where Mel and I had our interview.

I thought I was interviewing Mel to see if I wanted to attend the school, but he was auditioning me to assess if he would accept me as a student!

In front of me was a device that recorded the level of my voice. He asked me to read a one-page script in my normal voice while watching the needles move on the meter indicator. He then told me to whisper it while continuing to be cognizant of the meter level. After that, he commanded me to chant it. Next, put a pencil (lengthwise) in my mouth and read it again. It all seemed very silly.

Then he asked me to read the script again in my normal voice. Well, I can tell you the difference was night and day as to how better my projection was. The needle moved with little effort. I was impressed. What I also didn't know until we went back into that main room was he had the microphone on so everyone in the school could hear me. How embarrassing!

This story is here to show how even the simplest of exercises can improve your voice projection. Try the pencil. Even when you slobber out the side of your mouth and sound like your tongue has been cut off, it is one of the best voice exercises. Find more exercises to try online, or hire a voice coach.

To learn how to be a better speaker, there is no better program to join than Toastmasters. Check Toastmasters International to find a group near you that is convenient to attend. Major centers have several groups spread throughout the municipality.

Toastmasters provides an opportunity to learn the basics of a good presentation, where you can practice in a safe environment and learn from critique. The meetings are regimented for format and time, another skill one needs when managing a radio show or podcast.

2.2 Purchase good recording equipment

What happens when you find a live performance of your favorite band on YouTube, but the audio is terrible? You do the same thing you do with every YouTube video that isn't good; you look for another link with better audio.

You know your audio is off when your voice sounds like you're recording from under a blanket. Ideally in a video, you want both a clear picture and great sound, but it is bad audio quality that people will forgive the least.

Always check your audio settings before you record something or go live on air. If your computer's built-in microphone or the one inside your webcam isn't making the cut, invest in a better quality microphone.

Sometimes when I do a live recording, even a video recording that is scripted, I'll notice a few "ums" and pauses that appear to magnify in the archived recording. They tend to distract from what is said on the recording.

If you're going to produce a lot of audio programming, audio editing software is a must. Smooth out the rough edges and make the show flow better. Take out those "ums" and pauses.

Research the free and paid editing programs to see which ones work best for your needs. If you're dabbling in audio as a hobby, free programs such as Audacity might suffice. If you're serious about audio and see it as a branch of your professional portfolio, invest in something better if there isn't a free program that does what you need it to do. I personally use Adobe Audition. Most paid software programs have a free trial period so you can test how it works.

3. Online Radio Broadcasts

Blogtalkradio is one of many platforms for setting up an online radio show. It is a call-in Internet broadcast in which the audience is required to use a computer and a telephone. An unlimited amount of listeners can tune in but only a maximum of five can be on a broadcast at the same time.

Planning a show does take some commitment. You must be there at the same time, on time, every week. If not, people will move on because they will get tired of waiting for you to show up.

The platform is diverse enough that, besides sharing throughout your networks, shows can be set up for an RSS (Real Simple Syndication) subscription service through Juice or iTunes. These are free Internet services you can sign up for, in which you can pick and choose what you want to listen to. RSS distributes updated web formats, such as news, audio, videos, and blogs. It's a great tool for content publishers to automatically syndicate their material. A subscriber receives the updates automatically without having to check in with the source.

While there is a possibility that your show might be featured on the site's main page, your marketing is up to you. Marketing a radio show is no different than marketing a podcast, book, or blog. It is about reaching your like-minded audience and connecting with people in the platforms that are discussed in this book.

Spreaker is another place online where you can upload your music tracks or broadcast live from mobile apps or a computer.

4. iTunes

iTunes is the Amazon of audio. If you create your own music, have a podcast, or do anything audio, this is the platform most people think of first. Note that you don't need to own an Apple device to listen to iTunes, or even load content onto it.

There are other ways to do it, but the video "Easiest Way to Make a Podcast (for iTunes)"[2] made my process of getting audio programming on iTunes quite seamless. First, open a Podomatic account. If you already have an iTunes account, you don't need anything new, except to log in when you're ready. It will take a couple of days for iTunes to respond with its approval of each podcast after you submit it. At the same time, you can point listeners to your PodOmatic account.

---

2 "Easiest Way to Make a Podcast (for iTunes), YouTube.com, accessed July 5, 2014. www.youtube.com/watch?v=q2IGvPk4E-s&feature=share&list=PLkGyRMpoaLb8nPy-4CBR3nFpS4b7pEsUx

9
YouTube

YouTube is the second largest search engine next to Google, and it is just for videos. People love videos. They're easy to use and they do the work for viewers — people just have to watch. They are entertaining, informational, and some are downright stupid. More and more, videos are the way people want to view their content. Who wants to read an instructional booklet when a video can show you how to do it step by step? It won't be long before we are watching all of our favorite TV shows and movies live on YouTube or a similar platform.

YouTube is a Google product. With Google+ integrating its Hangouts with YouTube, delivering information by video is only going to grow. (For more information about Google+ Hangouts, see Chapter 10.)

If you have a Google ID, you can automatically log into YouTube. Note that every Gmail account comes with a channel. Figure 15 is a screenshot of "Virtual Newsmakers," my YouTube channel with Cynthia K. Seymour.

Figure 15

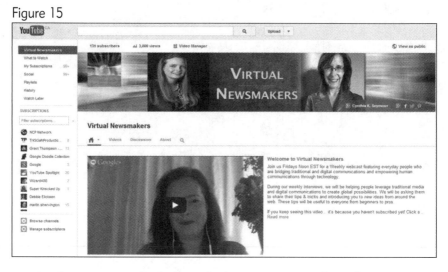

In the past, most of YouTube's commenters have been notorious for rude and awful behavior. The comments were an embarrassment to read and downright hateful. Then Google changed its settings so you had to be logged into a Google+ account in order to comment. It was the corporation's way of toning down the garbage.

A video with 200 to 250 hits is considered good, even though everyone is looking for the same success as the Volkswagen Super Bowl commercial: The Force.

The YouTube network houses nearly every artist one can possibly think of. To prove it, I challenge you to think of a singer or star you remember from childhood, one that few people may have heard of — it doesn't matter how old you are or what country you were raised in — and search for them on YouTube. A video will appear and you'll be able to take a trip down memory lane. There will be very few exceptions, that is, artists you won't be able to find on YouTube.

People are visual beings, especially our younger generations. Here is another challenge: The next time you walk into a trendy coffee house and you see a 20-something looking at his or her laptop or tablet, besides Facebook, what is he or she looking at? It is probably a video.

1. Make the YouTube Platform Work for You

Like any other social profile, take the time to complete your You-Tube profile. Do a periodic audit to ensure your information and the links are up to date. This is a free marketing tool, another on-line résumé or website where you can tell the world who you are and what you do.

YouTube is evolving and continually adding features and set-tings to help its users. You can create your own videos directly on the YouTube platform, upload a video from your computer, or broadcast a live Google+ Hangout on Air. Uploads from your computer can take a bit of time, depending on the strength of your Internet connection and the size of the upload, but the platform is relatively fast.

When you add a video to your channel, use tags and keywords that best describe how you want people to find your video. The one keyword you do want to add is your own name. Consider the following: "If I Google my name, will this video show up?" You want your name to show up in search engines so you can build a positive digital footprint.

When you first log into YouTube with your Google ID, if you look at the top right-hand corner, there is a circle gear icon you can click for a drop-down menu. Here you'll find the Dashboard, Video Manager, and YouTube Settings.

Click Dashboard and a new menu will appear along the left-hand side of the page. The community settings is where you can manage video comments and respond to messages in your inbox. Under the Channel settings, go to the advanced line and click to add channel keywords. This is how you want your channel to be found. For example, I have two YouTube channels under my name. One is dedicated to the information that appears in this book, so my keywords include social media, digital media, and transmedia. My other channel is sports related, so those keyword settings are sports, hockey, and National Hockey League.

If you go back up to that right-hand corner and click your email address, a drop-down menu shows YouTube settings on the left and you have direct access to your Google profile on the right. Click My Channel to optimize your profile for when someone visits your channel.

Your Google+ photo should be your profile photo. Add a background photo that relates to your channel's editorial guidelines. The About tab is where you will add a description of your channel. What types of videos do you plan on showing? Is your channel willy-nilly in its content or do you have a specific content angle?

In the settings you can choose to monetize your videos in the Features section of your channel settings. These are the video ads you see in other YouTube content. All you need to do is click the "Enable" button under Monetization. Don't quit your day job, because unless your videos receive tons of views, any checks you might receive from YouTube will be minimal, if there are any at all.

"Sub for sub" is a term for trading subscriptions with another YouTuber. You can help build subscriptions for your channel by subscribing to someone else's channel if that person subscribes to yours. It is a form of cross-promotion. Usually you would ask for the subscription and offer one in return.

When you do upload a video, optimize it by adding as much information as possible as to what the video is about in the description area. Have a good title that is searchable on its own. Look at the description area like a blog entry. Add contact links and as much information as possible. This will also show up on your Google+ page.

Be a thoughtful YouTuber and engage with the community. If you watched a music video you liked, hit the "like" button, share it on your other platforms, and make a comment on why you liked the video or thank the author for uploading it. These comments and the video will also show up on your Google+ page so that community has an opportunity to see and comment on it as well. Tell people you subscribed to them, either in the YouTube comments or on another platform.

Choose to make a video public, private, or unlisted. Public means anyone surfing the Web can find your video through your name, your channel name, your Google+ profile, the topic, or the keywords you created.

Because you can share a video with a link, rather than trying to email a file that is too big for the servers to handle, you might use the private settings to upload a video that is proprietary or personal (e.g., about your child's graduation). These videos can only be seen by you and anyone you allow to see them (with a link).

They will not show up in a search engine or in any public area of YouTube, including your channel. Anyone you share the link with will need to have a Google account in order to view it. No one can view the video unless you've added them to the viewing list, which means they can't share the link.

An unlisted video means anyone with the link can have access to it, whether they are a Google account holder or not. Anyone with the link can view it, but the video won't show up in the public areas of YouTube, unless someone added it to a public playlist, then it is possible it can still be seen.

All these settings can be a part of your marketing package. For example, a private message adds a personal touch if you are selling download packages, or to a new member who signs up for your online fitness program.

Videos can easily be shared across many of the social platforms by using the icons, or copying and pasting the link below them or at the top of the web page. Next to the "Share This Video" option is "Embed." This gives you a code to insert into a blog or website, so the video can be viewed inside of that platform. Once your video is uploaded and optimized, you can still make changes, and even delete it. Go into the Video Manager and click the "edit" button.

A company can make YouTube its recruiting tool, using short clips of one to two minutes. Consider clips of actual job tasks, showing employees working in a specific position, such as videos of a rigger or drywall specialist. The videos could talk about safety precautions and why they are important; or how a company protects the environment such as discussing steps to reducing waste.

If your target is a younger demographic for jobs, use younger employees to act in the videos. Have a plumber take a handheld camera onsite to talk about what he does, and what is needed for the job. Connect on the personal side of the company and its involvement in the community. Show staff members volunteering. There are lots of ways for any business to use YouTube as a résumé.

Sometimes an unpolished video connects with an audience better than the expensive professional video. It all depends on the purpose. The unpolished video keeps it real. For celebrities, besides song videos, fans like raw, uncut clips that show a more personal side from behind the scenes. Lady Gaga[1] has done this a lot.

1 "Eh, Eh (Nothing Else I Can Say) (Behind the Scenes)," YouTube.com, accessed July 5, 2014. http://youtu.be/zZ8GTIyi7e0

YouTube is a platform that artists, media, celebrities, and people of all walks have used to send out a strong message of change. Here are some examples:

- Madonna: Art for Freedom Project[2]

- TrueStoryASA (Adam Saleh and Sheikh Akbar): Meet a Muslim Person[3]

- cosmikdebris: The Magic Hockey Helmet[4]

- charstarlene TV: I Forgot My Phone[5]

Erik Qualman is one of the first to have produced videos about the merits of social media on his Socialnomics09 channel.[6] His Social Media Revolution video[7] is well used by social media advocates.

"I was out beating the drum about why everyone should have social media. I'd say this is important. I'd be sitting there for an hour talking until I was blue in the face not getting anywhere. I thought, man, I don't know what I have to do to get these people's attention. Then I thought: I've got to use what I'm talking about. I have to use social media. I posted a three- to four-minute YouTube video with a lot of statistics. All of a sudden, now I had everyone's attention that it wasn't just for teenagers. This stuff was going to revolutionize the way we did business and how we lived. I had to do it out of necessity. I wish I could say that I had this great business plan. I needed a tool because what I was doing wasn't working."

YouTube is a community, a marketing tool, and a concert hall. It is where you can meet people with like-minded tastes and develop friendships. You can receive visual instruction on how to clean the sensor valve of a furnace. It is where you can relive your favorite concert. It offers the platform to showcase who you are in a visual medium. So if you're an author, what a great place for a book trailer.

2 "Secret Project Revolution," YouTube.com, accessed July 5, 2014. www.youtube.com/watch?v=uXfXrl4K2D4&feature=youtu.be
3 "Meet a Muslim Person," YouTube.com, accessed July 5, 2014. www.youtube.com/watch?v= Z4U1dWtmHBM&list=PLkGyRMpoaLb966MV9gSUA5krcMtc6q2PO&feature=share&index=4
4 "The Magic Hockey Helmet," YouTube.com, accessed July 5, 2014. www.youtube.com/watch?v=rWjBvcfhRX0&feature=youtu.be
5 "I Forgot My Phone," YouTube.com, accessed July 5, 2014. www.youtube.com/watch?v= OINa46HeWg8&feature=share&list=PLkGyRMpoaLb966MV9gSUA5krcMtc6q2PO&index=5
6 Socialnomics Channel, YouTube.com, accessed July 5, 2014. www.youtube.com/user/Socialnomics09/about
7 "Social Media Revolution," YouTube.com, accessed July 5, 2014. www.youtube.com/watch?v=sIFYPQjYhv8&feature=youtu.be

10
Webcasts and Webinars

It is a beautiful time in history to be working in visual arts. Can't sell your project to the Food Network, HBO, or NBC? No problem. Try Netflix, Hulu, and Amazon. They don't want it either? Try Vimeo or YouTube; these two platforms also have an on-demand feature where developers can upload and sell their projects independently.

Chris Yates of Huddle Productions[1] made the full shift from traditional broadcasting to webcasting in 2007. His media is video-driven social media for business owners and brands that turns customers into fans.

Like most media types, he began humbly. "If you remember *Wayne's World*, I did that in college. I was awful, but I loved it. I started working in TV and worked everywhere out of college," Yates says.

He broadcast on CNN, CBS, NBC, and FOX. In 2007, he pitched an idea to Budweiser. "It was called Bud Light's Ultimate Tailgate. At the time, I was still naive on the social media stuff. I hedged my bet. We created a 30-minute TV show that aired on FOX TV Southwest, bought the air time, and produced it."

1 Huddle Productions, accessed July 5, 2014. www.huddleproductions.com

Yates traveled to football stadiums and created videos of him interviewing fans and featuring the craziest tailgaters. The show developed a following and when approached by someone about it, he would remark he was glad they watched it on FOX. The viewers would respond to say they didn't know it was on television. They saw it on YouTube and Facebook.

"After a while, I started realizing, there's a business here. TV viewership was dying and everyone was going online. The next year, I shifted the entire focus to strictly online."

They submitted the program for an Emmy award and were up against FOX, NBC, ABC, CBS, and MSNBC. "We beat them all. It goes to show you, it really doesn't matter what station you're on. It matters how you put stuff together. I think, if you're talented, it really doesn't matter where you're doing it."

1. Google+ Hangouts on Air

Google+ Hangouts on Air is a free platform that comes with a Google+ account. You can create your own video show or use it for meetings — both business and personal. It offers a face-to-face discussion with up to nine other people at a time who can be physically located anywhere in the world. It is Skype on steroids!

You need a Google account, an Internet connection, plus video and audio features in your device to broadcast on Google+ Hangouts on Air. If you're not familiar with this platform, Martin Shervington has a wonderful tutorial on YouTube.[2] You can also find out more information from Google.[3]

To get your feet wet before you schedule your own show, watch and participate in other Hangouts. In the beginning, I looked for shows that were of some interest to me, where I might learn something about social media or other business topics. Then I gathered the courage to find a live, open Hangout where anyone was invited. Note that you won't always know what the discussion is about until you get in.

There are people who schedule regular or impromptu open Hangouts. They just wait to see who shows up and then the discussion becomes whatever they decide at that moment. Go ahead and join one. A cool thing that can happen is you make new friends.

2 Martin Sherrington on YouTube, YouTube.com, accessed July 5, 2014.
 www.youtube.com/user/MartinShervington
3 Google Hangouts On Air, Google+, accessed July 5, 2014.
 www.google.com/+/learnmore/hangouts/onair.html

Through a couple of these, I met an Internet thought-leader from Tokyo, and a student from Brazil I kept in touch with, hung out with again, and connected with in other platforms.

Google+ Hangouts on Air can be live and in the public forum, or held privately. The actual setup of a Hangout is the same for both. The only difference is whether you click the "Start Broadcast" button for pushing it live. Don't click if you want to keep the Hangout private.

You might use the live Hangout to:

- Set up an educational video that showcases your business. For example, if you are a computer programmer you may have a program titled "How to find the right antivirus program".

- Prepare a visual portfolio of your work, such as an acting reel or a video introduction of what your company is about.

- Interview someone.

- Share a vignette to illustrate a message.

- A tutorial on how to do something.

A private Hangout might be for:

- Brainstorming with your colleagues across the globe.

- Interviewing long-distance candidates for a job.

- Business meetings.

- In lieu of a telephone call with your best friend.

- An open invitation to anyone on Google to join so you can meet new people.

What we have done for Virtual Newsmakers is set up a link for our show, then we give our guests the inside link via email, Google chat, or Facebook, whatever is the preferred choice by our guest for communication. The guest can click that link and jump into the Hangout directly, or from the invitation that shows up in Google+ and Gmail.

Having the inside link is important in case one of the participants bounces out of the broadcast, which can happen because of streaming and Internet issues. When someone does fall out, the audience doesn't really notice because the large screen is focused on the person who is talking. The rest of the participants are shown in the thumbnails below it (see Figure 16). The person that did drop off can return without calling attention to the fact he or she left the broadcast. Chances are the viewer didn't notice.

Figure 16

Besides the inside link, there is also a public link for the people outside of the Hangout. That is the one you would spread through your networks. Put the public link on all your social networks right before the broadcast so your followers can watch the broadcast live. If they want to watch it later, they can use the same link to watch it from the event page or they can go directly to YouTube.

The beauty of a Google+ Hangout is that the show is automatically synched with your YouTube channel. After the broadcast, go into YouTube and add tags, a thumbnail picture, and edit the description or title as needed. What you put into the Hangout when you set it up will be what shows up on YouTube.

Here's how to set up a Google+ Hangout session:

1. Install the Google+ plugin[4]

---

4 Google+ Plugin for Hangouts, accessed July 5, 2014. https://tools.google.com/dlpage/hangoutplugin

2. Switch browsers if you have difficulties getting in (e.g., from Chrome to Firefox).

3. Go to your Google+ page and look for the button "Start a Hangout on Air." (See Figure 17.)

4. Title your Hangout session so it reflects your discussion (e.g., "How to Write a Book").

5. Add a description. The more detail you can add the better for the search optimization from the YouTube archive of the broadcast. Treat the description like a blog. Check out the descriptions on Virtual Newsmakers for an example.[5] Include links and contact information so people can find you after the broadcast. There is no such thing as too much information. Don't worry if your description is 250 to 300 words. If you only pen a couple of paragraphs, make the message as succinct as possible.

6. Schedule your broadcast for "now" or "later." You will be asked for a date and time, plus an end time. (See Figure 18.)

7. Invite specific people from your circle or open it to the public.

8. Check your lighting. In front of a window, your face could appear darker due to the backlighting. Try pointing an incandescent desk lamp toward your face.

9. Prevent audio interference by using a simple set of earphones which will help prevent you from hearing feedback.

10. Try and simplify your background as much as possible. You want the camera to focus mainly on you. As you can see in Figure 16, I've tried to unclutter my background with an organized bookshelf behind me to minimize distractions for the viewers. Ideally, the backdrop would be a blank wall or screen so the camera will focus only on you, rather than get confused as to which object/person is the main focus.

Once you hit the Share button on the setup page, the event page will open (see Figure 19). Add photographs, links, and instructions for your viewers, or chat with them in the feed underneath the video box.

If someone wants to watch the event, he or she will view it by clicking the play button inside the video box. As the administrator

---

5 Virtual Newsmakers, YouTube.com, accessed July 5, 2014. www.youtube.com/user/VirtualNewsmakers

Figure 17

Hangouts On Air

Start a Hangout On Air

Broadcast your convers
YouTube. Learn more

Figure 18

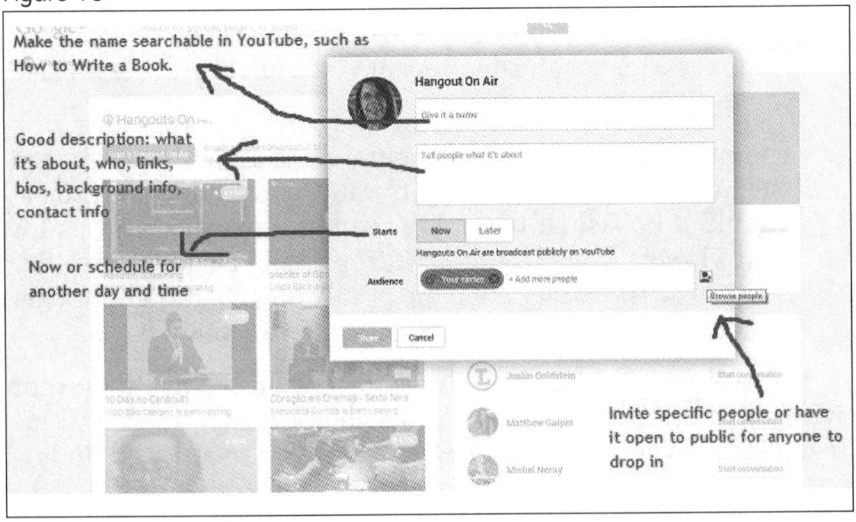

Make the name searchable in YouTube, such as
How to Write a Book.

Good description: what
it's about, who, links,
bios, background info,
contact info

Now or schedule for
another day and time

Hangout On Air

Give it a name

Tell people what it's about

Starts   Now   Later

Hangouts On Air are broadcast publicly on YouTube

Audience   Your circles   + Add more people

Browse people

Share   Cancel

Justin Goldstein

Matthew Galpin

Michel Neray

Invite specific people or have
it open to public for anyone to
drop in

setting up the Hangout, you will click the blue Start button (see bottom left corner in Figure 19) which will bring you inside the Hangout to allow you to get ready to broadcast.

A Google Hangout is only "on air" (live) when you hit the Start Broadcast button. You can chat all you want behind the scenes before and after a broadcast or never hit the start button at all. If you do start the broadcast, just hit the "End Broadcast" button in the same spot to end it.

Figure 19

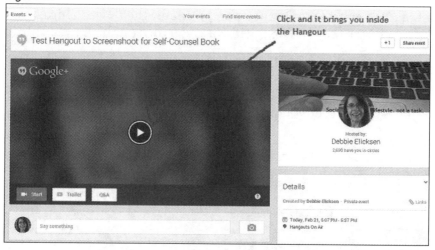

In Figure 20, the link at the very top of the Hangout box is the inside (private) link you can share with the guests you want to bring into the show. This would not be a public link, unless you want anyone to drop in. You can have a maximum of ten people in a Hangout at a time.

Hover the mouse to the left side until the icons show up. The following numbered list corresponds to the numbers in Figure 20:

1. The Hangout Toolbox is the seventh icon from the top. On your first Hangout, it might take longer to download the toolbox when you click on it.

2. On the opposite side, you'll see another menu. Go to the top, find the circle with the head silhouette and click for the Lower Third.

3. Your name (what your Google+ account is under) will show up here, but you can add your company name, website address, or Twitter handle. Note that you have limited character space. To check on how it appears (it will appear backwards only to you as it is in Figure 20), click your thumbnail at the bottom of the Hangout (if there is more than one person inside) to see your picture in the big screen. You can also check the angle of your camera and center yourself with your background. Click the thumbnail again so your image doesn't remain in the larger screen when others join the Hangout.

4. You can use more than one preset for the Lower Third. Just choose one by clicking it when you turn on the Lower Third.

5. For any Hangout, turn the button to "On" to make the Lower Third appear. By default, it will be whatever your Google+ profile shows. If you want to change it, click the saved preset you prefer to use instead.

Figure 20

When you mouse over the middle at the top, you'll see six icons pop up. Beginning from the left of Figure 21, the buttons do the following:

- Invite people: You can bring more people into your Hangout with a Google invite.

Figure 21

- Mute microphone: If someone has a lot of background noise that is distracting or muffling someone else's speaking, you can mute his or her microphone and then turn it on again when it is his or her time to speak. If people have trouble hearing you, check this setting to make sure you have not muted yourself.

- Turn camera off: If you have to get up and leave the broadcast, but you want to come back in, instead of having an empty chair in the screen, click off your camera and the audience will see your Google+ profile picture.

- Adjust bandwidth: Make sure you have as much bandwidth as you can get to keep from dropping off or having streaming issues.

- Settings: This is where you adjust your video and audio settings. If you have more than one camera or microphone, let the Hangout know which one to use. If you're having audio and video problems, you can also check these settings to make sure you're connected properly.

- Leave call: When the broadcast is over (although you can still talk with the people inside the broadcast, even if it is not live) you can hang up on the broadcast using this telephone icon or by closing out of the Hangout screen.

Check out the rest of the icons on the left side to see what also may apply. You won't need to use all of them, but go ahead and test the settings. The second icon from the top is the private chat box, which enables you to talk and post links for the people inside the Hangout. This will not show up live.

The green arrow icon is screenshare. If you have a PowerPoint or photo gallery on your computer for a show and tell, this function will let you show what you see on your computer — live. Hitting the screenshare button again turns off the function.

2. Spreecast

Spreecast is a social video platform where people connect via web conversations. Similar to Google+ Hangouts, you can broadcast live or have a private meeting. People use the platform to discuss topics of all sorts. Bloggers, journalists, and celebrities, among everyday people, create shows to foster opinions from others, educate, and entertain. Spreecasts can be used to connect with clients, talk about upcoming events and product launches, and also to help build a social presence.

When you set up a Spreecast profile, be sure to add links to your other networks and write a good description about you and your channel. Don't make people work at learning who you are.

You can log into Spreecast with a Twitter, LinkedIn, or Facebook account. When you log into Spreecast, you can see what shows are currently live and on air. Find shows to watch either by searching for specific hosts or topics, or checking out what is popular and trending.

You can have up to four people in a Spreecast as seen in Figure 22.

Your Spreecast profile lists how many shows you've been associated with as a guest, on camera, produced, viewed, and more. The page in Figure 23 is where you would also see scheduled shows, when you have set them up.

Create a Spreecast any time in advance and the link will be available for pre-promotion. The same link is where the recording is housed. Share the Spreecast before, during, and after on Facebook, Twitter, LinkedIn, and Google+. Embed the broadcast into your website or blog, and viewers can watch the show from there — both live and once it's recorded.

Figure 24 shows where the live and recorded link is located. The chat box actually transforms into its own community. The icons of the people participating (watching and onscreen) show up below the broadcast box. Anyone watching the show can ask a question and participate in the chat box. They can also request to come on air and it is up to the producer to let them onscreen.

In Figure 25, at the top, when you mouse over your photograph, you'll see a drop-down menu where you can edit your profile and change your settings. Click the plus sign in the green circle to create a new show.

Figure 22

Figure 23

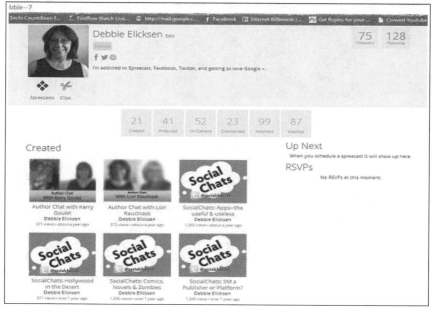

Figure 24

The online chat in the lower right-hand corner is where you can see who else is online in your Spreecast community. Underneath that Spreecast toolbar is Live & Upcoming and Popular & Trending. Click on either of those links to search for other shows to watch or participate in.

Figure 25

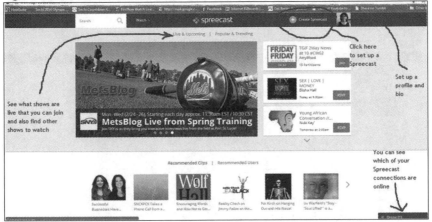

As you see in Figure 26, when you click the Create Spreecast button, a callout box appears. You have limited character space, so choose your words wisely, and pick words that will help your Spreecast get found. Here are some examples:

- SocialChats: Comics, novels, and zombies

- Description: Arcana comics: examples of how comics/ graphic novels/sci-fi are setting trends in publishing.

- Category: Books & Authors

- Tags: publishing, comics, apps, Debbie Elicksen, Cynthia K. Seymour, Comics in General, Tonya Scholz, Arcana Comics

- SocialChats: Apps <— the useful & useless

- Description: App talk. Free versus paid. Interactive versus static. Are they what you expect?

- Category: Technology

- Tags: apps, Susy Rosado, Debbie Elicksen, Tonya Scholz, transmedia

Figure 26

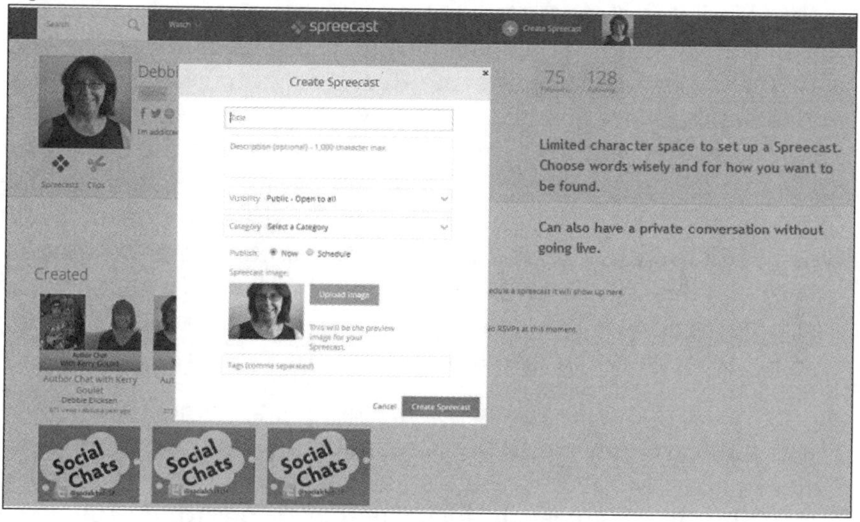

Figure 27 shows Spreecast asking for me to check my camera and audio settings to make sure they are both working. You may have more than one camera or microphone connected to your device, so you want to make sure you're using the one that will work best with your online settings. For example, while I have separate webcams for my desktop and laptop, instead of using the microphone in the camera, I use a separate microphone that I plug into my device.

Figure 27

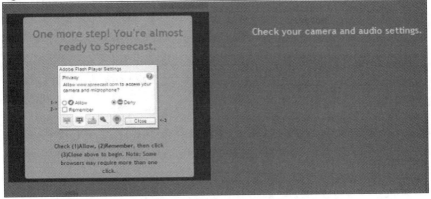

The person who creates the Spreecast is automatically a producer. You can invite others to come in as producers, which gives them complete access to the back end of the Spreecast and its settings. The "producer chat" is where you can have a conversation with the other producers of the Spreecast. For example, if you noticed someone viewing the show was a known spammer, you might point that out in the producer chat and alert the other producers. If there are more than four people in the Spreecast, one person can say he or she is stepping out or the fifth person might type in the producer chat that he or she wants to answer a question or expand on a discussion. The "public chat" is where anyone watching the show live can chime in. What happens in the live chat is the viewers can also talk to each other.

Invite as many people as you would like to come on the Spreecast, but only four can be onscreen at the same time. Viewers, who can also use the live chat, can ask questions. They go into the queue and the producer decides whether or not to put the question on air. If so, then the question shows at the bottom of the broadcast box. If there are a lot of viewers and questions, it helps to have more than one producer so you don't miss a potential conversation.

In Figure 28, which is a private Spreecast, a link to the public live chat is visible. The box for the producer chat is private.

If there is a Spreecast issue and you require help, the developers can live chat with you from the lower right-hand corner and walk you through issues while you're on the air or about to go on air.

Figure 28

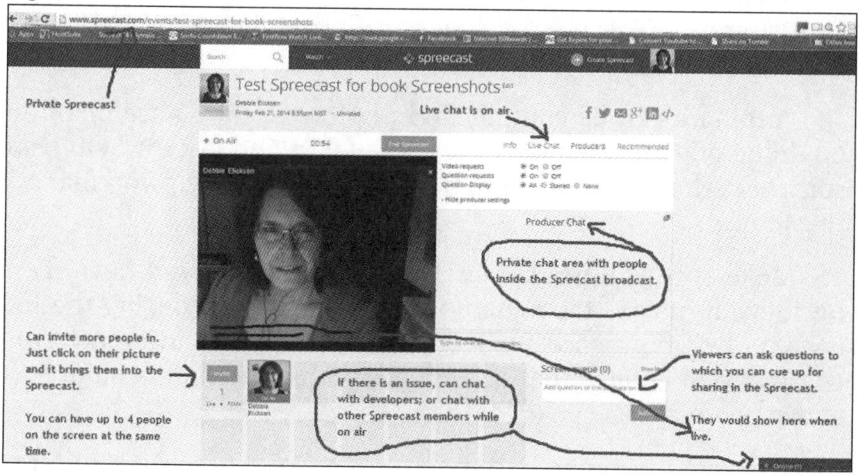

To end a broadcast, click the "End Broadcast" button, and it will ask you if you are sure, just in case the button was clicked by mistake.

As soon as the broadcast ends, a screen appears with post-production settings. Use the embed codes and add the Spreecast to a website or blog. Also share your broadcast further by pulling out and sharing specific clips from the show. You can share from within Spreecast, directly to Facebook, Twitter, Google+, and LinkedIn.

3. Webinars

The webinar platform is different than a Hangout or a Spreecast. There are both audio and visual components to a webinar; however, the audio is either via telephone or through a computer's speakers. The visual is usually a PowerPoint or shared screen presentation. There is also an interactive module. Participants can ask questions through a chat message. There are presentation options a speaker can use, such as a whiteboard that participants can also write on.

To host a webinar, you need to team up with a webinar service, which provides the web conferencing tools required to conduct a successful event. Most of these services offer a trial period to test out their platforms, but these services are not usually free.

Some of the better known hosts are Cisco WebEx, Webinars OnAir, and GoToWebinar. You can find reviews[6] online for the different webinar companies.[7]

Webinars can be complicated platforms. If you are planning on doing one, do a couple of test runs first and ask for help from someone who has done them before or who can help you manage the show.

Make sure you print your PowerPoint slides and have them beside you in case the slide portion fails to work during the live event. Always prepare for technological issues and create your presentation as such that if it ended up that the slides couldn't be shown, you can still go on with the show.

The worst webinar I attended wasted more than ten minutes of time because the presenter was upset over his PowerPoint not being available. He clearly didn't print off his slides and he didn't have any notes beside him that would have allowed him to continue.

Webinars are a difficult platform in that if you are used to live feedback during a presentation, here you are talking to dead air. There are people tuned in, but you can't hear them or see them.

What is the one thing we do when we are nervous and are not getting feedback? We whiz through the material. Try and slow down so that you're not faced with killing time at the end of the event.

---

6 "A Survey of 6 Top Webinar Platforms for Business," BUX, accessed July 5, 2014.
  http://abetteruserexperience.com/2013/01/a-survey-of-6-top-webinar-platforms-for-business
7 "Reviews of the Best Webinar Services," No1Reviews.com, accessed July 5, 2014.
  http://webinar-services.no1reviews.com

11
Social Media Overview

"The cost of your social media education is going to be great but if you don't invest in your education now, it will be costlier later."

Michael Gass

You may have already decided, without having tried any of the social media platforms, that you hate social media and your business doesn't need it. *You* may not need it, but what about your customers and the people who might want to hire you? What if *they* need it? You may change your mind after reading the following 2013 statistics Jeff Bullas[1] gathered from the *Search Engine Journal*:

- Facebook is the number one influencer of purchases for 47 percent of Americans.

- Facebook has 1.15 billion active monthly users.

- Google+ has 359 million active users.

---

1 Jeff Bullas, accessed July 5, 2014. www.jeffbullas.com

- Twitter has 215 million active users.

- 71 percent of users access social media from a mobile device (Adobe 2013 Mobile Consumer Survey).

Consider the percentage of people who use social media:

- 18–29 year olds: 89 percent

- 30–49 year olds: 72 percent

- 50–60 year olds: 60 percent

- 65 and older: 43 percent

Do you still think you don't need social media? The bottom line of marketing 101 is to be where your customers are. These are the most important networks to be in:

- Facebook

- Twitter

- Google+

- LinkedIn

Facebook may not be the best fit for your business. Maybe Google+ makes more sense. Or YouTube. Go to where you feel comfortable engaging and playing with the platform until you get it right. Know these platforms will continually evolve. Algorithms and navigation will change. However, the heart of the programs will remain the same.

To sell computers, a computer company must stay relevant and up to date with everything that is new in technology. What would your perception be if that company still sold Windows ME? Perception *is* reality. If you're not dabbling in Internet media, now is the time to begin. Social media platforms were not created for advertisers; they exist for the consumers.

The good news is that small firms can compete with the big guys. The Internet has leveled the playing field. However, it is not a passive arrangement. Everyone must work at it. If you are unique, distinctive, authentic, passionate, and you have great content, you should do all right.

It doesn't matter what demographic, which country, or what a person's interests are, everyone is desperate to connect. People want to feel heard and valued. That is why connecting with your followers is social currency.

1. Build a Social Media Platform

"Experiment at first when building a platform. Listen. Identify individuals to follow. First posts may not get noticed. Don't take things too seriously. Perfection is the opposite of social. Be authentic," said Niklas Myhr, of Chapman University.

Even if you're starting from scratch, you have to begin somewhere. Don't worry about being everywhere at once. Go at your own pace. Maybe add a profile to as many networks as possible at the same time then build out from there. Or focus on one or two and really work them until your community blossoms.

You don't have to learn everything in one take. Build your network systematically and learn the platforms in increments. Talk directly to your demographic for ideas. Pay attention to what your favorite thought-leaders share. Connect with like-minded individuals, those who are known in your industry, and those you respect and admire. When you have the right people in your network, you will have a lot of great material to curate from your own newsfeeds.

Keep redefining your sites. Facebook, Twitter, and LinkedIn must be updated daily in order for you to keep being seen. Change your photograph and time line photos. When you sign up for new networks, go back and add those links to all your other sites. All three can be linked together so that one status update can update all three sites (Facebook, Twitter, and LinkedIn). However, these platforms aren't always synonymous with each other. Adding unique content to the post could extend its reach further.

No matter what platforms you choose to be in, make sure your profile is filled out in detail. Consider it like a résumé. Don't fill out your name, maybe a company name, and have no picture then expect that to create a following. These are some examples of what *not* to do:

1. **Facebook:** When friends try to engage, give no response. Is this a real person? There is no profile picture. What are you hiding? Are you a spammer, phisher, or creep? We have a lot of mutual friends, I see, but your profile tells me you're just a troll. (See Figure 29.)

Figure 29

2. **Google:** When you sign up for Gmail, you automatically get a Google+ account. Complete your profile so it doesn't look like Figure 30. Interestingly, this person's popularity outranks his profile. He has more than 600 people he could be turning into disciples.

Having no profile picture, or an avatar as a picture, makes people think this person is standing in the corner of the room of a party with his back towards the room, arms crossed, and saying, "Leave me alone." This actually seems to be the case if there are 647 at his party and he's only bothered to acknowledge 12 of them. This is a viral résumé opportunity lost.

Figure 30

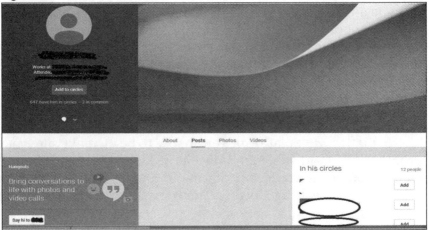

3. **LinkedIn:** People join LinkedIn for the business connections. There is nothing to see in Figure 31. Also note the spelling error in the job title. Really?

Figure 31

4. **Twitter:** Figure 32 is what a spammer looks like. Not knowing how to work this platform meant this person's account had also been infiltrated by a spammer. This showed up in direct messages with a phishing link. The person did not respond when I advised him his Twitter account had been hacked.

Figure 32

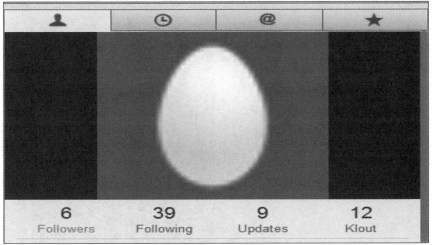

If any of your profiles look like these, fix them now or remove yourself from the platform. Don't waste the Internet space.

People connect with people. Don't post your logo or book cover. Make sure your photograph is a reasonable likeness of you. A picture of you and your dog or your child would not be appropriate on LinkedIn or a Facebook business page, unless your business is a pet store, veterinary clinic, or has something to do with children.

There is a fair time commitment required to set up your networks, and then to maintain them. That is the price of free. You could enlist a professional to do the work for you, but every profile should appear as if it is personally yours.

Take a look at Richard Branson on Google+ and Eminem on Facebook (see Figures 33 and 34). There is a strong chance they have someone else posting on their behalf, but when you look at their posts and engagement, it looks as if they are personally responding. The posts are personal, in their voices, and congruent with who you expect them to be as people.

Figure 33

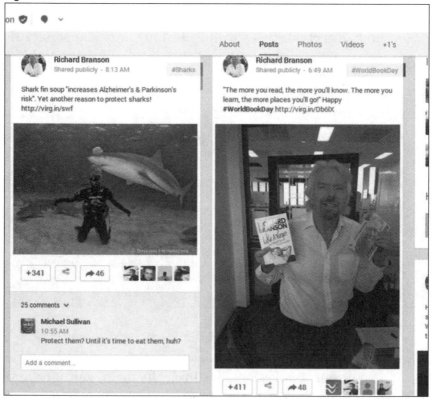

Figure 34

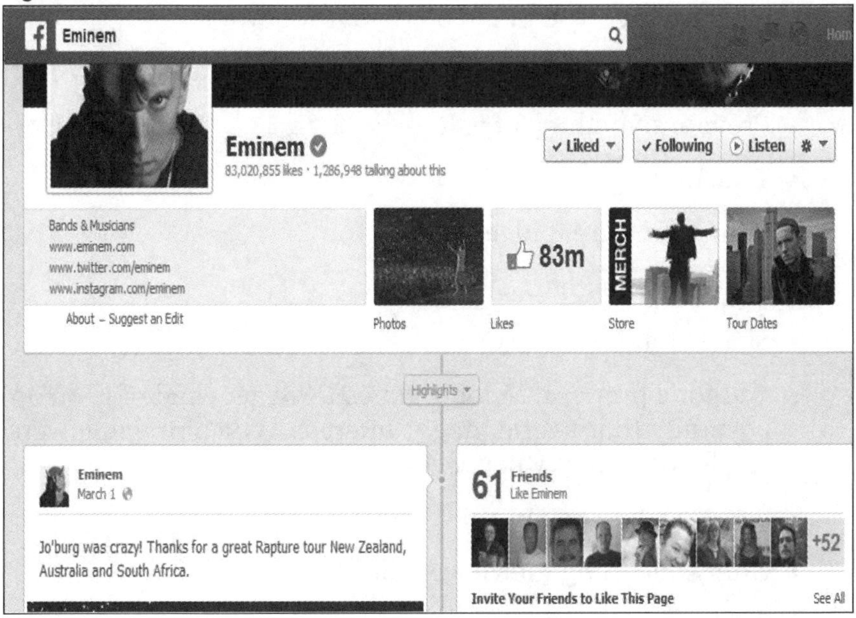

Social networks can be very fast-paced. A lot of things can be thrown at you at once. It is essential to stay on top of it. Note that social media isn't "one size fits all." What you post in Facebook may not look as cool in Twitter. What you post in Twitter may not pop in Google+.

Here are some things you could do:

- Share research results.

- Refer someone.

- Offer a how-to tip.

- Provide a strategy for something.

- Share new trends impacting an industry.

- Respond to someone's post.

- Recognize someone.

- Connect two or more business people.

- Share a personal story to save someone some grief. For example, if you downloaded something from what looked to be a legitimate website, but it turned out to be a knock-off phishing site, you might alert your followers.

- Post some inspiration (e.g., story, quote, video, picture).
- Provide something of value.
- Teach.
- Share some great ideas.
- Share a news item.
- Share your blog entry.
- Call for a proposal. A lot of times I will get wind of a job opportunity that I think might interest some of my followers, so I'll post it to my networks.
- Share a white paper.
- Offer something the viewers need.
- Offer something for free.

Most important is to be consistent with your message and repeat these actions regularly.

1.1 Share your knowledge

> *"The first thing you need to do in social is listen. Nurture the community."*
>
> RIC DRAGON

Traditional methods of advertising and marketing do not work on the Internet. Traditional or old marketing uses interruption to reach the unreachable; new marketing is set up to reach the reachable.

Online, success breeds imitation; and you get back what you put in. Social networks are windows of transparency. It is virtually impossible to be false or deceptive without everyone catching on.

Seriously, unless your name is Jennifer Lawrence or Brad Pitt, we don't really want to know that you are sitting on your deck having a coffee with the cat on your lap — unless you post a really cool photo or you know your network really does care about that.

Also, don't oversell something. Okay, we get it. You sell Amway. That doesn't give you the license to spam my wall and say, "Hey, check out this great opportunity." Instead, be a source of information. Post something on your own wall that makes the rest of us take notice such as "Here are 12 uses for Amway dish detergent you may not have realized." Don't spam. Yes, you can potentially reach hundreds of thousands of people in one post, but it doesn't mean you should if you have nothing viable to say.

Sharing without asking for a reciprocal task is considered social capital. Each of those tasks gets deposited into your social media bank of respect.

Draw people to you by posting cool and interesting stuff. Marketer Lawrence Bland[2] suggested, "Post 20 tweets of meat then you can post a link to your products." But do it tactfully, not in that typical "buy my stuff" language. Invite people as your guests to an event or share the Amazon link to your book: "It's finally here! Now I can drink!" If you are interesting enough, people will eventually check out what you do.

This may seem crazy, but the more you give away, the more business you get. Content is king. If you give away a great tip, and someone who uses it experiences a 10 percent improvement in what he or she is doing, that adds to your "I better follow this guy" cred.

Kim Beasley is the founder and producer of KimLive.TV[3], which brings interactive live-streaming video to the masses using Google+ Hangouts on Air. She specializes in integrating other social media networks, such as YouTube, and publishes recorded shows on Facebook, LinkedIn, Twitter, and Pinterest.

When it comes to Internet marketing, Beasley is very good. She has helped many of her clients get into segments on HuffPost Live.

Beasley has a warning for people who do Internet marketing wrong: "If you hawk your wares, it puts people off."

The attitude to have is to share your knowledge. Do this by sharing a blog post. Keep creating and look for opportunities to syndicate. Most important: Be promotable. Allow other websites to pull your content into their site. Bring in other writers to guest post on your blog and encourage them to share. Become a coauthor.

---

2 Lawrence Bland, Twitter.com, accessed July 6, 2014. https://twitter.com/LawrenceBland
3 KimLive.TV, accessed July 6, 2014. http://kimlive.tv/

In these platforms, in order to be open to receive, you have to be able to give. Sharing is a two-way street. There is no greater gift than a shared post in social media.

Allow for easy sharing of information. You want your content to go viral. If you write an article, blog post, or post a photograph, allow people to re-pin, retweet, and re-share. You never know who is going to see it and what kind of opportunity it might create.

There is a hotel that has a front desk person who communicates with guests on Twitter to advise them of places to eat and what to visit in the city. He's funny, too. Imagine how guests feel when he makes them laugh and provides good value that impacts their stay. Do you think they will come back? Of course they will. How many people do you think they will tell about the experience? That is social media return on investment.

1.2 Attract, engage, convert

"Think who, not how many."

SETH GODIN

Don't think about how many followers you have. Instead, look at your engagement with those followers. Social media is a place to create a conversation about a topic or issue, test ideas, create a buzz, and capitalize on your uniqueness.

Yes, there are many services that proclaim you can have a gazillion followers overnight. How many of those are fake accounts? How many are following you because they perceive you to be interesting and worthy of following? The numbers don't matter if the followers are robots.

I can't say it enough. Those snaky services that sell followers are a waste of your time and money. If you do get 2,000 followers from these people, sure, it looks nice on your profile. Chances are most of them will be spammers like the person you bought them from. These are not people who have been handpicked just for your industry. What they will do is spam your legitimate followers to sell the same service.

You are better off cultivating 50 disciples from your naturally found contacts. These are the people who will personally help you spread your business.

When you do have legitimate followers, if you continuously talk about your company or product, you will turn them off. People will get bored and leave you if that's all you do. They'll also block you if you spam their Facebook walls, LinkedIn inboxes, and Twitter feeds enough times.

What will work is a true conversation. Talk about things that people care about. Put a human face on your company. Don't hide behind a logo. Listen. Participate. Tell a story. Create an experience. Be an educator.

If you are promoting a business, people are not going to get as excited about the brand as they will a person representing the brand. We know that Peter Cashmore of Mashable[4] and Richard Branson[5] of Virgin are the brand as much as their companies are.

Inside Google+ there are numerous Google employees who put a face on that brand. They're not the Richard Branson of the company or a household name, but they are real people behind the scenes who make the company run. They are in plain sight for customer service. If you've ever had a question about Google, you can ask them directly. They are actively posting useable information, too.

Be genuine. People engaged in social media can spot a phony a mile away. If you don't use a real photograph, it isn't a stretch before someone calls out your avatar as a fake. If you aren't man or woman enough to post a picture, then what else are you hiding?

You only post what you want other people to see. If you don't post anything, you're not interested in marketing, period. Leave the venue and go home.

1.3 Driving traffic

The Director of Community, Tim McDonald,[6] from the *Huffington Post* offers the following formula for an optimal social media presence:

- 1/3 content creation

- 1/3 curation

- 1/3 engagement

4 "Pete Cashmore of Mashable: The Sage of Social Media," Success.com, accessed July 6, 2014.
   www.success.com/article/pete-cashmore-of-mashable-the-sage-of-social-media
5 Richard Branson, Wikipedia.org, accessed July 6, 2014. http://en.wikipedia.org/wiki/Richard_Branson
6 Entries by Tim McDonald, The Huffington Post, accessed July 6, 2014.
   www.huffingtonpost.com/tim-mcdonald

Publishing your own content is a no-brainer. If you get really good at curation, finding good and relevant content, then people are drawn to you as one of their news sources. Engagement is what really makes things move in social media. We're not talking about dropping a creepy "hi" into someone's Google+ messages. Real conversations develop strong connections and create loyal disciples.

Whether you develop your own content or add your insight to a curated link, one post can be spread in several unique ways.

For example, at Virtual Newsmakers, we set up a show with a guest, and then share the event link with others: "Did you know we have ... on the show? Here's the show link ... ." That can then be pushed out further into a pre-event press release, which can also be spread throughout various networks.

Another way is to draw from our guest's information — a blog post he or she wrote or a product launch — and send that with the show link to all your networks. Once the show has aired, the video gets shared with all the networks. A series of tweets can be created from the guest's quotes. Along with the show link and the guest's Twitter handle, the tweets get scheduled over time, and keep circulating on Twitter. Screenshots of the video are shared with each network, with a quote from the guest and link to the show. A blog post created from the show that includes screenshots and the embedded video of the show is shared to all the networks. One video or blog has the potential to be spread at least ten different ways.

1.4 Geolocation

I would personally recommend not geolocating (adding a location) to any of your social networks. Do you really want the world to know where you are at all times? When you add a location to some networks, many times it goes beyond the actual city, but right to the exact building location.

Your network doesn't really need to know you posted that meme of Grumpy Cat from your home computer in Albuquerque, New Mexico, at house number 123 on such and such a street. If you're a female living alone or with your five-year-old daughter ... you get where I'm going here. That's like going to the packed movie premiere and just as the commercials end, before the previews, standing in front of the screen with a megaphone and telling the audience: "My house is empty right now and I live at this address. Please rob me."

Turn off the geotagging in your smartphone, too, while you're at it. Note that digital cameras also have geotagging data that can stay with your photos, so you should turn off that feature as well.

2. It's a Lifestyle, Not a Job

It always amazes me how many companies think that web design and social media go together in a job description. Or that a person must have a Bachelor of Arts degree or any other prerequisite, other than actually having social media cred. I've seen companies hire and fire "social media experts" who had all those academic qualifications, because when it came down to the actual job of managing social media, they failed spectacularly.

Consider a social media community manager to be similar to a ghostwriter. The following is a list of qualities and skills required to get the best out of social media. You either need to develop them for yourself or hire someone who already has them. This kind of experience does not come with a university degree:

- Strong communication and literacy skills.

- Strong people skills.

- Ability to write blog posts, guest articles, emails, proposals, social content, and messages to fit any medium.

- Outgoing, friendly, and relatable online presence.

- Comfortable interacting with people (a natural networker).

- Good judgment, level-headed.

- Good at curating.

- Have an idea what to share, how to share, and when to share.

- Determine the best ways to handle feedback and how to respond in an appropriate fashion.

- Know the audience and be able to effectively converse with them and see their perspective.

- Be available to respond in a reasonable time (ideally within 24 hours or faster).

- Be the face of the brand and a brand ambassador.

- Create a customer experience.

- Manage multiple platforms and track feedback.
- Flexibility.
- Be able to do multiple job responsibilities (e.g., marketing, public relations, and communications).
- Use analytics to determine what is working and not working.
- Enable and empower your community, create conversations.

3. Helping Others Can Turn Business Relationships into Friendships

When you really play in the platforms, people can feel like they know you and sometimes you'll even meet offline. When you do, there may be none of that awkward first meeting stuff going on.

My friend Dan sent me a Facebook friend request because he saw we had a mutual interest in lacrosse. He was a fan and I had been reporting on the game at the time. We had a couple of mutual connections that were lacrosse related. We got to know each other over time through our posts. When I had a local book signing, he made an effort to show up. It was the first time we met face-to-face.

We had a lot of common interests besides lacrosse; one was music. I saw that he never missed a concert, so when I had been left with an unused ticket to a concert in another city that I wanted to see, I sent Dan a Facebook message and asked if he wanted to come. He did, and we drove three hours, had supper, watched the six-hour concert, and drove three hours back — all in one day. Months later, he had an unused ticket to a local concert and asked me if I wanted to go. I did and we had a great time listening to great music.

A while back I received a LinkedIn message from a contact I didn't really know, who asked if he could introduce me to someone. I agreed to the introduction to Urs who lived in Hong Kong. He hired me to help him manufacture his book. All of our communication was via email, with a couple of Skype calls in between. After the book was published, I introduced him to Tonya, a colleague with whom I was cohosting a web show. She ended up interviewing him on one of her other shows.

These examples show that you never know how your social media connections will help you, but they will.

12
Google+

Google+ is a mixture of personal and business. It's not quite as informal as Facebook, but it's not as formal as LinkedIn, either. It hovers somewhere in between. Google+ is all about community. What and how you post in another network is reworked in Google+ to maximize your social cred.

Being in Google+ will push your search engine optimization to a higher ranking in Google. The company won't even try to deny this fact.

Sarah Matista wrote a post called "Benefits of Google Authorship for You and Your Business."[1] In it, she quotes Google CEO Eric Schmidt: "Within search results, information tied to verified online profiles will be ranked higher than content without such verification, which will result in most users naturally clicking on the top (verified) results."

What that means is if you have an active Google+ profile, you will rank higher than someone who does not, especially if you verify your Google+ profile with your website blog.

---

1 "Benefits of Google Authorship for You and Your Business," SocialMediaToday, accessed July 6, 2014 http://socialmediatoday.com/smatista/2200396/benefits-google-authorship-you-and-your-business-infographic

1. Create a Google+ Profile

Let's begin by creating a Google+ Profile:

1. Open www.gmail.com (or www.google.com).

2. Use the prompts to set up a Gmail account. Pick an email address that most closely reflects you or your business. It might take several attempts to find one that isn't already taken. Choose a password; this is your login password to all Google accounts, which includes Google+, YouTube, Google Drive, and more.

3. You can skip the telephone authorization for now.

4. Personalize your email settings by adding a signature and background photo.

5. Open Google+ and set up your profile. When you are in, and you mouse over "Home," a drop-down menu will appear; click "Profile." In Profile, click "About" and complete as many details as possible. Make it real and build a comprehensive profile.

See Figure 35 for Google platforms in a Chrome browser.

Figure 35

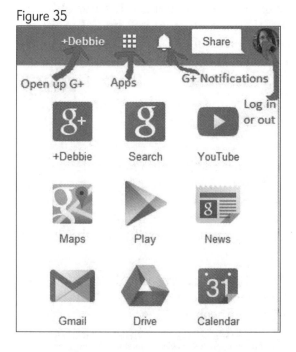

Similar to Facebook, you should use a cover photo and a profile picture to give life to the profile. Use a real photograph of yourself. If you want to use an avatar, do it on the cover picture.

What do you do? That is the question your profile needs to answer. Don't make people ask you. Make it easy to see and be easy to communicate with. List your links to other platforms and websites — include *all* of them. Make the Google+ profile your backup system for all things you.

2. Elements That Make a Good Post

This is a site you want to post something in every day. Take a look at the "What's Hot" feed and get a sense for what people like to share.

There are elements that make a good post in Google+. Think of your post like a blog. If you only post once a day, make it a good one.

Tagging is important. Do this if you want someone specific to see this post. If you are re-sharing a post, tag the person you got the post from, and also tag the person who initiated the post, if it's a different person. Be gracious. If you carry a conversation under a post, it's okay to tag the person's name you are talking to. For example, +Self-Counsel Press, you guys rock!

While Google Search does categorize posts by topics and the questions they answer, use keyword hashtags to contribute to the post's searchability. Add the #hashtag at the #bottom of the #post. See Martin Shervington's example of sharing someone else's post (Figure 36) for a guideline.

Here are some tips for posting:

- Bolding text is created by adding an asterisk (*) before and after what you want bold. Shervington would have done this: *I wasn't going to mention it, but ... *

- To include someone in the post, put a plus (+) sign by his or her name like Shervington tagged +FOX 11 Los Angeles, +Maria Quiban, +Stan Bush, and +Stormy Henderson.

- The +58 under the image equals how many people liked this post. (See Figure 37.)

Figure 36

martin shervington
Shared publicly · Feb 24, 2014

I wasn't going to mention it, but...
Just did a hangout with +FOX 11 Los Angeles and the lovely +Maria Quiban,
and chatted about stand-up comedy with Sir Ben Kingsley.
Standard Monday ;)
h/t +Stan Bush, and thanks +Stormy Henderson

Stormy Henderson originally shared:
I got to video chat with Sir Ben Kingsley this morning, thanks to +Maria
Quiban and +FOX 11 Los Angeles!

He was promoting his new short film, All Hail the King, where he resumes his
character from +Iron Man 3.

Watch the interview at http://youtu.be/Pyf87bjLs5Q.
Show less

+58

22 comments ∨

Maria Quiban Yesterday 3:40 PM +1
will do! +Stuart O'Neill. See you back in the hangout! :)

Figure 37

- The middle icon is for sharing the post on other networks. This may show up because of an add-on app I have on my desktop if it doesn't show up for you. I also have an app that lets me hover over the corner of the photo and a Pin It box that will show up, which enables me to share this picture and post it on Pinterest.

- The right-pointing arrow is how you would share to your feed in Google+, which is what Shervington did with Stormy Henderson's original post; he then added his own commentary.

3. Circle-icious

When you follow people on Google+, you add them to a circle. They don't see what circle you have them in, only that you are following them.

It takes time to build a following. First, go into your people settings to see who is in Google+ from your Gmail connections, YouTube, or do a search for someone specific or an industry. Look for people who will add value to your news feed. It's easy to unfollow people if you change your mind. You can also mute posts or block them.

Don't make the mistake some of us made at the beginning and tried to fix after following 2,000 people. Break down your circles into topics that make sense to you. If you add everyone to the same circle, that's okay, but it makes it difficult to cull people.

For example, if you are a musician following other musicians, you could have circles named: music (which would be the catch-all), alternative, rock, jazz, drummers, guitarists, and managers. The more specific your circles are, the easier it will be to personalize your content so it makes sense to the right people (see Figure 38). You can also add a single person to as many circles as you want.

The home feed shows posts from the people you are following. Communicate with them in the comment box or like and share

Figure 38

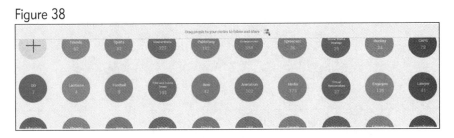

their posts. When you post, you can customize who sees it. You may only want certain circles to see it or only a single person. You can also have a conversation with just one person without anyone else being able to see it. It still shows up in your profile feed.

Google communities are a great way to meet new people, besides shared circles and connecting with people you know. Communities are like one big discussion board. Some are better than others. If it is not serving you or adding value, you can always leave.

4. Google+ Trolls

Both women and men get Google+ trolls. You'll know one when you see it. Figure 39 is an example of a Google+ troll:

Figure 39

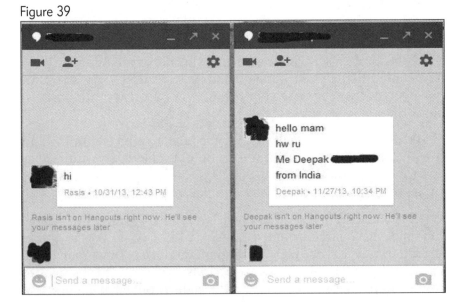

These are two instant messages that popped up. One of them kept messaging every couple of minutes with just a "hi."

This is not what engaging with others looks like. It's annoying and creepy, so don't do it. Almost 100 percent of the time these people are not even connected to you, so that means they are phishers or spammers. The only thing to do with them is to block them, and you do that by clicking on the little gear icon in the top right-hand corner.

5. Launching a Music Career on Google

Heather Fay[2] is a great example of how you can use digital media to create a fan base. What she has done as a musician can certainly translate to publishing a book.

At college age, Heather Fay considered herself a late bloomer with starting a music career. Even so, she just picked up a guitar and "strung" with it. You could have called her a closet musician. She really didn't release any music until much later. Why? It's personal.

Many authors can relate. An artist feels naked and vulnerable at the thought of releasing his or her work. It's terrifying.

Fay did try the traditional audience, but to reach the larger crowds, a musician has to tour. She was a young mother with a two-year-old and she couldn't justify leaving her family for the road.

Enter Google+ Hangouts on Air. Here was a platform that let Fay reach the world without sacrificing time with her child. It also gave her a way to connect with musicians all across the globe.

She showed up regularly and developed a following. With the help of her production team (her husband), she created music videos and posted them to YouTube. She joined other musicians on Google+ and hung out on air with Artists in the Plus,[3] which is an online music festival.

When it came time to create her CD *Cherish the Broken*, she used the crowdfunding site Indiegogo to raise money to produce it. One of her Google+ followers created the cover.

While her downloadable music is available through the digital channels iTunes and Google Play, when someone purchases a physical CD, she personally sends it out so she can attach a message to each one.

2 Heather Fay, accessed July 6, 2014. http://heatherfay.net/
3 Artists in the Plus, accessed July 6, 2014. www.artistsintheplus.com

Fay used Google+ to tease fans with clips, artwork, and even document the process of creating her CD. She was so grateful to the people who supported her, she created a series of heartfelt thank-you videos.

You may think that a YouTube musician wouldn't have the opportunity to network or catch the eye of the A-list music community. Think again. She was noticed by the one and only Bono, who asked her to join U2, Bruce Springsteen, Mumford & Sons, Muse, Green Day, and many more on ONE.org's Ultimate Protest Song Spotify album for campaign Agit8. The Agit8 campaign is a movement to bring back the spirit of the protest song. Fay performed the Bruce Hornsby song, "The Way It Is."

13
Facebook

Facebook CEO and founder Mark Zuckerberg has completely turned the world upside down. He didn't just bring more than a billion people together on one platform; he was the first to deliver a social network to Wall Street. While Facebook is considered more social than all of the other networks, a lot of business gets done there.

Facebook is seemingly a main communication tool with teenagers and 20-somethings, next to texting. If you have children who are this age, you already know they don't answer their cell phones or emails, but you'll get a response in real time when you Facebook or text them.

Back in 2007, a dear friend told me about this site and encouraged me to join. I was reluctant. My fear of Internet growlies — adware, viruses, and all that junk that comes with e-cards and email spam — made me hold off. Then I watched *Reliable Sources* with Howard Kurtz on CNN and he spoke with two guests about their experiences on Facebook. After the show, I decided that if Facebook was good enough for these three journalists, it was good enough for me, so I signed up for Facebook. To say that it didn't consume my time for the next few days would be a lie.

1. Facebook Tips

Facebook's design and settings have evolved over the years and the platform keeps changing. Even so, the basic template is still there — the premise of how the social network operates.

Your profile photo is the one everyone sees when you post on other people's walls or message them. I recommend you use your picture here, mainly because it helps those who are looking to connect with you on Facebook.

Your cover photo is the larger photo on your personal page. It is up to you how many times, if ever, you change your photos. This picture might reflect something about your personality.

Make sure you have a decent profile, including photographs, and not stock images. At the very least, list your employment and job description, or what you would be looking for should an opportunity come to you.

The Facebook wall (also known as the "Timeline") is where all your posts show up. It is possible to post on other people's walls directly or by tagging them in a post, but use discretion. Don't market on other people's walls, and don't tag people on every post, especially if you tag more than one person.

You can see who is online to message. If you do send someone a direct message, even if it shows he or she is online, it doesn't mean that person will respond immediately, or at all. He or she could have Facebook open, be doing other things, or maybe he or she is away from the computer. Protocol says the person will respond as soon as he or she can. A regular Facebook user will often respond within the hour if he or she is not doing something else away from the platform, or by the end of the day.

Direct messages show up as instant messages, too. This can be a quicker way to reach someone urgently rather than email. If the person has a smartphone, depending on how his or her system is set up, a Facebook message notification might show right away, whereas the person may have to log into his or her email account from a browser to get those messages.

1.1 Create a fan page

A personal Facebook account is required before setting up a fan page (also known as a Facebook page). The page can be for a business, for a specific interest, or for someone who has too many followers on his or her personal page (you can friend a maximum of 5,000 people).

Facebook pages need a lot of time and maintenance to attract and engage with a community. Josh Henderson (John Ross Ewing on the television series *Dallas*) has the right idea.[1] He is personal and engaging. He asks questions of his fans, posts lots of pictures, including behind the scenes stuff. He gets feedback on each episode. He adds reminders as to when the next show will be. He'll offer commentary — in character — from the storyline. He also keeps the page fresh during the off-season with information from his other projects.

Figure 40 is the Facebook fan page for Virtual Newsmakers. As you can see, we are still building our community.

Initially, you would invite people in your personal account to "Like" the page (but *not* as a direct message — you do it from the page). The About section should have a good description on what your page is about and links to your other networks. Administrators of the page can choose to post as the page or as themselves.

You can add more features to your page (e.g., photos, events, notes, videos, reviews, newsletter sign up). When you, as an administrator, go to like another person's page, you can also choose to like it as yourself or as your page.

1.2 Invite others to your Facebook group

The Facebook group is similar to a Facebook fan page, but with fewer features. One of the more annoying aspects of a group profile is that the owner can add people without asking; whereas on a Facebook page, the owner invites people to like it or connect with it.

I have a Facebook Group[2] I started before Facebook introduced "Pages," and because it still seems to offer some value to the members, I've kept it. I can see a link to a relevant article on LinkedIn or Twitter, and choose to share it on my personal timeline, one of the pages I manage, or a group page. I do post on the

---

1 Josh Henderson, Facebook.com, accessed July 7, 2014. www.facebook.com/JoshBHenderson
2 Book Publishing 101, Facebook.com, accessed July 7, 2014. www.facebook.com/groups/102682486146

Figure 40

group page from time to time, and I have my Network Blog syndi-cation posts shared with the group because I feel I need to respect the people who asked to join it.

If I add any future platforms to Facebook, it will likely be in the form of a Page, just because it seems more advanced.

When you do get added to a group page you don't want to be-long to, go into that group and click the wheel for the scroll-down menu. From there you can click "Leave Group." (See Figure 41.)

Figure 41

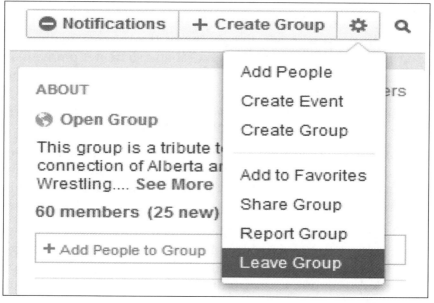

There are a lot of people who whine about privacy issues. Yes, I said whine. If you are serious about marketing and want people to connect with you, and if you plan on being anywhere on the Internet, privacy is out the window. It's like a famous movie star not wanting anyone to recognize or talk to him or her. You can't have it both ways. That said, you can adjust the settings so only your connections, or some of your connections, can see your posts.

2. Give Purpose to Your Facebook Pages

My goal on Facebook is to inspire, offer some nuggets of information, encourage people to think, and give them a laugh. If I do my job right, they will come back and ultimately, they'll take a look at what I do and then they'll refer me or support some of my projects.

My personal Facebook page gets more traction than any of my business pages, probably because that is where I spend most of my effort. That is what I talk about the most when I talk about "my Facebook." In my work, business *is* personal. However, as a business, if you prefer to work your business page over personal, the following philosophy still applies.

Figure out what you want from your Facebook community. Before you can expect to receive it, you have to give it. Be real, show up regularly, and don't "feature dump" all over the place. Tell people about what you're doing, or post a link to your Amazon page, but do so with discretion. Post something every day. Engage with those who are already there. If you see something in your Home feed that you like, "Like" it and share it. Comment on other posts. Do a bit of this every day to get noticed and build your following. If you are constantly "selling," consistently negative, or downright rude you probably won't build a healthy following. People will soon tire of it and unfriend you.

You can hide specific posts, and block certain people from seeing some of your shares, but for the most part, if you are not active and open to new connections, don't expect any Facebook love in return.

If you write to people you are not connected to and say anything to the effect of "buy my stuff," expect to be blocked and reported for spam. If you "inbox" a whole whack of people you are connected to in one message, they may not report you for spam (it's harsh and can result in you losing your account) but they will likely leave the conversation. If this behavior persists and someone doesn't speak up to slap you, you might end up unfriended, blocked, or hidden from future view. Just because it is easy, does not mean you should do it. (When I got reprimanded for doing something like this in the beginning, I was grateful because it was an act of kindness to teach me to right my ways.)

Use Facebook to build relationships. As with all networks, become a real member of a community and add value to it. If you are a company, people are more likely to connect with a brand when a real person seems to be behind it. If that brand adds value, then word will spread.

Coca-Cola works its community with real conversations around the brand. One example is a clip that was posted with a picture of a polar bear along with a link for donations. The text that went with the picture gave fans an interesting tip as well as a call to action (in this case, "donate"): "Did you know polar bears have such a strong sense of smell they can detect food from miles away? Help support these amazing animals, text MATCH1 to 45678 to donate $5 to WWF and we'll match your donation!"

Add personality to your business page. Talk to people as if they are in the same room, like you are hosting them in your home for dinner. Networking with people to gain their trust takes some elbow grease. Start saving the bacon residue from the pan.

Here are some Facebook business page protocols:

- Allow people to engage — open settings for wall posts and discussions.

- Link to your company's causes.

- Point to authoritative third-party reviews (e.g., PEW Research Center reports).

- Publish customer ratings.

- Post videos and photographs.

- Encourage discussions on hot topics.

- Connect prospective customers to each other.

- Link to websites and pages of interest that your company endorses.

- Add interesting content, such as tidbits on operations.

- Add a tab for a contact capture form for recruiting or sign-ups to e-newsletters and blogs.

- Use Facebook impression ads to test drive different ads to get people to "Like" the Facebook page. These ads can be specifically targeted, right down to the community, likes, and demographics of users. The ads operate on pay-per-click and can be scheduled to a specific time frame.

- Post events and jobs.

3. Networking Takes Time

I built my list of friends by connecting with people who were already on Facebook from my email address book by using the Find Friends feature. Then I went to each of those friends' profiles and looked at their lists to see who I knew and connected with them. It didn't take long before I reached my first 100 and it grew from there.

Because my networking philosophy is "you don't know who people know," the ones who made the most difference were those I didn't know. I've had the best time getting to know them, and it is clear that if it were not for Facebook, we would have never met. Some of them give me referrals, some I've met in person and I've gone to events with, and with others I conduct business. Many have turned into good friends and acquaintances. I have had large projects where the bulk of communication was done via Facebook.

Sometimes one of those friend requests looks a bit off — sort of creepy, maybe a fake. You don't have to friend him or her. Or, friend the person and you'll know immediately if it's a fake. The person will either message you with a pledge of love or spam your wall. Then you can unfriend the person or block and report for spam.

Most of the people you don't know will turn out to be OK — even great. Think of it like going to a conference. You may not know everybody, but do you turn your back and dis people just because you don't know them? If you don't read anything else from this book read this: **You don't know who people know.**

That person who looks like he or she is not important, of whom you might have heard rumors, who doesn't work in the industry you are targeting — he or she could be the gatekeeper to your next big break, to the love of your life, or to your next business partner.

Nothing worthwhile is going to happen at the snap of a finger. Networking can be a slow process. Make it better by really making sure your profile is continuously updated and includes the latest links to your other social sites and blogs. Make it easy for people to connect with you.

When people click your "About" section, they should see your work history, what you specialize in, and what product or service you produce. If you're looking for work, it should show the type of work you are looking for. Consider this simple profile a résumé that works without you when you least expect it.

I was sending out a weekly newsletter through email, which netted me a few referrals. I eventually realized those referrals were happening less. The number of referrals I was receiving from Facebook warranted that I pay more attention to that platform. When I stopped the e-newsletter, maybe five people noticed.

14
Twitter

"Twitter is an alternative messaging service."

HOWARD KURTZ
(FOX News, former host of
CNN Reliable Sources)

Twitter is a real-time information network. It is where you get the news you want when you want it, 24/7. It's microblogging in 140 characters or less. It's not so much about friend connections, but rather like-minded followers. Twitter is the most effective source for breaking news and to learn what is happening.

Before you send out your first tweet, note that Twitter is similar to other media (e.g., Google+, Facebook) in that one main thought should cross your mind before you hit the tweet button: Is this post offering any value to the community? What are you personally going to do to improve the content viewers see on the Internet?

You wouldn't think that one could conduct business on a platform with such limited text talk. However, Twitter has replaced the telephone call to establish a cold lead. For Virtual Newsmakers, my cohost Cynthia Seymour noticed Josh Rock was an account manager at CollegeRecruiter.com. Because she thought he would be a good for our show, she reached out to Rock through Twitter to introduce herself. Her initial tweet tagged me and @VirtualNewsShow to establish the "hello." A series of tweets later, we booked him on the show.[1]

Figure 42

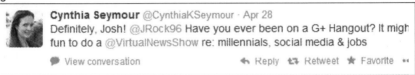

Cynthia Seymour @CynthiaKSeymour · Apr 28
Definitely, Josh! @JRock96 Have you ever been on a G+ Hangout? It migh fun to do a @VirtualNewsShow re: millennials, social media & jobs

💬 View conversation   ↩ Reply   ⭐ Retweet   ★ Favorite ··

Like in any online network, you don't know who is watching. Shama Kabani (the author of *The Zen of Social Media Marketing*) created her book when there wasn't really anything on the market that talked about social media. She self-published it as an ebook and used Twitter to tell people about it. A publishing agent saw her one of her tweets and began to follow her. The agent reached out to her and she was soon offered a publishing contract.

Twitter protocol means you don't spam. Sadly, you do see your fair share of it. The key to engaging others to follow you on Twitter is to give people meaty tips and interesting links, or play-by-play commentary on sports, awards shows, political coverage, storms, and basically any event worldwide. Responding to people who try to talk to you, either in your feed or through direct messages, will also help you increase your following.

Erik Qualman, the author of *Socialnomics*, reported in his book that Gary Vaynerchuk grew a family business from $4 million to $50 million using social media. Vaynerchuck spent:

- $15,000 in direct mail = 200 new customers

- $7,500 in billboard ads = 300 new customers

- $0 in Twitter = 1,800 new customers

1 "Virtual Newsmakers features Josh Rock," YouTube.com, accessed July 6, 2014.
www.youtube.com/watch?v=WNLwsYj2Zhg

1. Set up a Twitter Account

The hardest part of Twitter is finding the right user name that works for you. The longer you wait to get a Twitter account, the more likely the name you want to use will already be taken. Think branding; think long-term when choosing a name. If possible, use your own name.

Once you secure a Twitter handle and sign up for an account, go to the settings and begin customizing. As with all your other social media platforms, make sure you complete your profile in as much detail as possible. You'll also want to dress up and personalize your background. You could have your Twitter background match the color scheme of your website and other social media venues and use the same profile and cover images. (See Figure 43.)

Figure 43

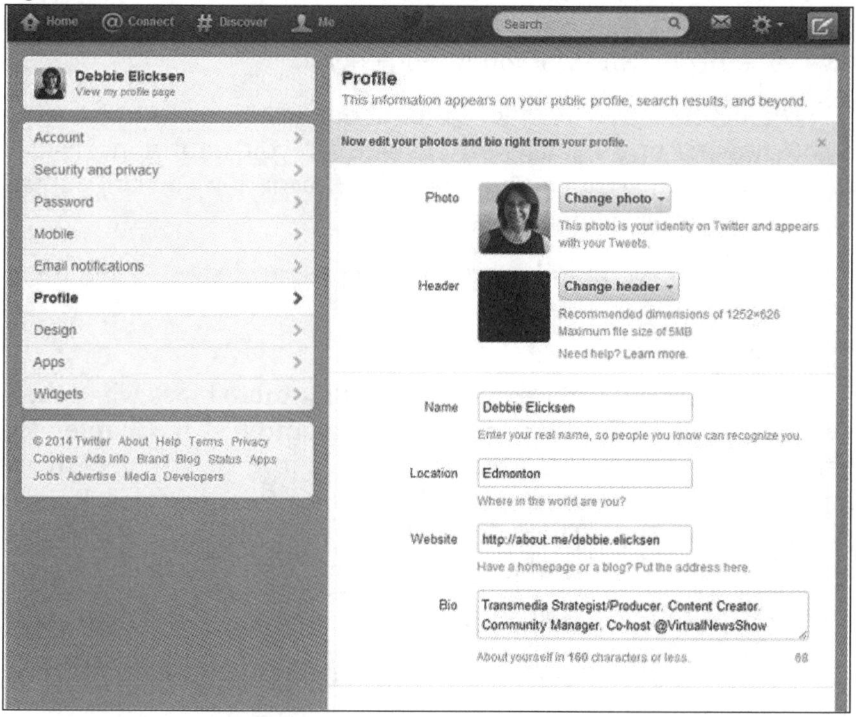

The same protocol about profile pictures works here as it does in Google+ and Facebook: Show that you are a real person by using your picture and not an avatar.

There is an option to privatize or "protect" your tweets. Quite frankly, I'm not sure why that option is even in Twitter. When you click this option, it means anyone who wants to follow or communicate with you has to ask your permission. It screams that you are completely unapproachable. You're the guy at the party with your entourage and no one can come inside your inner circle without your approval. What happens when you see that guy? You forget about him and never give him another thought.

Please don't protect your tweets. What you have to say is just not that important. If you use this function, you might as well not bother setting up an account and wasting a user name someone else might want. There, I said it.

Besides finding who you know on Twitter from your email account, check out who other people are following. You may find someone with similar interests who might add value to your Twitter newsfeed. It also helps build your following because there is always someone who will follow you back.

When you follow people, think about what type of news you want showing up in your Twitter feed. Do you want nonsensical ramblings or an actual newsfeed with information you can curate for your other social networks or blog?

To manage your followers, add people to lists to customize how you find them. This is similar to Google+ where you add people to specific circles.

There will be Twitter handles you will want to block when they show up as spammers or phishers (as mentioned in Chapter 11, using the egg icon instead of a photo). Their feeds also give them away). You'll see the same tweet and link sent to hundreds of people at the same time. The link may be either a full link or a Twitter-shrunken link. Their feed might look something like this:

- @yourtwitterhandle: Check this out!!!!! ow.ly/i/5Bn6C

- @SelfCounsel: Check this out!!!!! ow.ly/i/5Bn6C

- @bookpublish101: Check this out!!!!! ow.ly/i/5Bn6C

- @anyothertwitterhandle @anothertwitterhandle: Check this out!!!!! ow.ly/i/5Bn6C

One of the common terms you hear in regards to Twitter is the hashtag. It's a fancy word for a number sign (#) in front of a word or phrase that is a key word. For example, if you are interested in finding out what people are saying about the #SuperBowl, it might already be trending, in which case you can click on the term and see the feed or you can put "SuperBowl" or "Super Bowl" into the search area.

Let's talk a bit about trends as this is also where hashtags come in. Trends can help you tap into conversations about certain topics. For example, the #yeg hashtag represents Edmonton, Alberta, Canada.

Say you're a Thunder Bay-based author who has been brought into Edmonton to do a book signing and talk about developing cohesiveness in a blended family. It's your first trip to Alberta and you know nothing about the city or its culture. By searching the #yeg hashtag, you can discover recent chatter about a number of topics that are related to the city. Maybe there is a large event going on at the same time as your event that might impact its turnout, or that you can incorporate into your talk to localize the topic. Or, you might notice there is a bad accident that will detour your cab ride to the venue, so in order to be on time, you'll know to leave your hotel a bit earlier.

Let's take a look at the tweets in Figure 44 so you can get a sense as to the elements of a tweet.

- @JMalks has posted an Instagram photo and is implying that spring has finally reached Edmonton (#yeg) so it is time to enjoy a bike ride. The hashtags he uses describe where he has taken his bike. YEG Retreat has retweeted his tweet, which may have been found by the use of the #yeg hashtag.

- @totalfilm also posted a photograph inside a ballroom at Cannes where he mentions that actors Jude Law and Chris Hemsworth are not in the shot, but nearby.

- @NBCSportsPR shows you how to market without selling.

- @citibank is a paid tweet, which is an advertisement that is cleverly disguised as a tweet. It is selling the company and stretches the envelope a tad more than @NBCSportsPR did on its tweet, but it isn't that annoying "buy my stuff" post you see in a lot of these mediums.

Figure 44

I admit that when I first opened a Twitter account, I wondered what the big deal was. I just didn't get it. I dabbled in it for a while, just enough to keep it active. I understand that it can seem overwhelming for people who are new to the platform. Add in that when you are following a lot of people, you can't keep up with the feed. If anyone is talking about you, it's difficult to scroll down and down and down as tweets keep coming in.

In Figure 45, the Home button takes you back to your main page, where your followers' feeds are. When you click #Discover, you'll see a collection of tweets that Twitter culled for your perusal, based on your interests, which the algorithms have gleaned from your activity and use of hashtags. The Me button takes you to your personal activity on the platform.

Notifications is where you can see if someone is trying to have a conversation with you, retweets, who has mentioned you in a tweet, who favorited a tweet, and who has followed you. It is common courtesy to acknowledge those who mention you in a tweet, as long as it isn't one of those spam tweets that were mentioned earlier in this chapter. You might even thank someone for retweeting (RTing) you.

Figure 45

2. Twitter Tips

Follow these tips to get the most out of your Twitter account:

- Tweet every day. Post original tweets, such as a quote, words of wisdom, or an opinion, and share a link (say something about the link so people don't ignore it as spam).

- Retweet other people's posts, but don't use their posts exclusively as your Twitter feed. Use a mixture of your own tweets and those of others.

- Use Twitter to help build awareness about an issue or project.

- Play around with the apps available. For example, you can embed your tweets on your website as well as link them to your LinkedIn and Facebook accounts.

- Follow people in your industry and others who are of interest to you. Retweet other tweets that mirror your philosophy, or that might be of interest to engage the Twittersphere.

- Respond to queries in a timely fashion. Twitter is in real-time so if you wait a week to respond to someone, he or she has probably moved on.

The most important tip is to be yourself, but beware of what you say. Once a tweet goes viral, it is impossible to take it back.

3. Twitter Management System

I mentioned that I didn't really "get" Twitter that well in the beginning. Then I was introduced to HootSuite. It blew my mind. I was shocked to discover how many people were trying to connect with me in my Twitter feed, but their messages were totally lost.

I immediately saw many lost opportunities. People were querying me about various topics and some of them might have led to something else if they were responded to in time. You never know where a tweet will take you.

HootSuite is a Twitter-management site, although you can manage other accounts with it, such as Facebook and LinkedIn, too. There are similar tools to help you manage Twitter and multiple social media networks and make your life easier such as TweetDeck and Bottlenose. Each of these sites are free to operate for up to five accounts. The paid versions offer the ability to connect more accounts and have greater options, such as better analytics.

Eric Qualman describes how a social media management tool works: "If you want to post something, say you find a great article that is appropriate for everybody across the social networks, then you just have to post it once and it goes to all those networks. It also gives you all the statistics you want. You can find out who retweeted you or who your biggest fans are."

I personally manage no fewer than five Twitter accounts, so HootSuite is a lifeline for me.

Figure 46 is screenshot of my free HootSuite feed. The first five tabs at the top are the accounts I manage. The others are streams I check in on from time to time — feeds from which I curate information. In this screenshot, my @debbieelicksen account is what you see:

- Column 1: Home feed is the newsfeed of all the profiles I follow.

- Column 2: Mentions are what makes a management system worthwhile. This is what alerted me to the bevy of individuals who were trying to start a conversation with me when I first signed up for this service. You can easily see who is talking to you in the newsfeed when they use your Twitter handle in part of their tweet.

- Column 3: Direct Messages are private messages. A lot of auto-responders show up here, which post spam-like messages intended to create a conversation with you when you follow someone. It might include, "Thanks for the follow, download my ebook, buy my stuff, follow me on Facebook ... ." Twitter rule: Don't do to others what you don't like seeing in your own feeds.

Column 4: Sent tweets shows you all your most recent tweets.

Figure 46

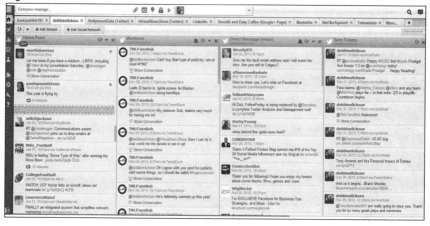

When you reply to a tweet, the person's Twitter handle (e.g., @Person'sHandle) will show up and then you fill in the blank. Add a link by pasting it inside the "add a link" box to shrink it so it doesn't take up so much space, an attachment (e.g., PDF, photograph), and send it at a specific time. (See Figure 47.)

Figure 47

Retweeting is considered social currency. If there is room, you can add some commentary, but always keep the retweet @whoever the originator is. Think of Twitter (and any other network feed) as a publisher. If you retweet something without crediting the original source, consider it a form of plagiarism.

The beauty of HootSuite is that you can schedule tweets to go out without you. If you manage Facebook and LinkedIn from it, you can also schedule posts to those platforms. I will power schedule tweets for three to four weeks at a time (see Figure 48).

Figure 48

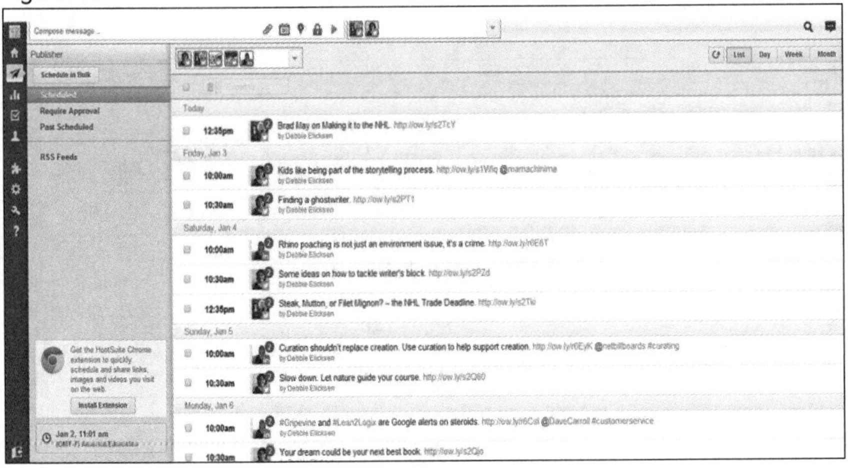
Compose message...
Publisher
Schedule in Bulk
Scheduled
Require Approval
Past Scheduled
RSS Feeds
List
Day
Week
Month
Today
12:35pm
Brad May on Making it to the NHL http://ow.ly/s2TcY
by Debbie Elicksen
Friday, Jan 3
10:00am
Kids like being part of the storytelling process. http://ow.ly/s1Wfq @roamachinima
10:30am
Finding a ghostwriter. http://ow.ly/s2PT1
Saturday, Jan 4
10:00am
Rhino poaching is not just an environment issue, it's a crime. http://ow.ly/r0E6T
10:30am
Some ideas on how to tackle writer's block. http://ow.ly/s2P2d
12:35pm
Steak, Mutton, or Filet Mignon? – the NHL Trade Deadline. http://ow.ly/s2Tki
Sunday, Jan 5
10:00am
Curation shouldn't replace creation. Use curation to help support creation. http://ow.ly/r6EyK @netbillboards #curating
10:30am
Slow down. Let nature guide your course. http://ow.ly/s2Q60
Monday, Jan 6
10:00am
#Grapevine and #Lean2Logix are Google alerts on steroids. http://ow.ly/r6Cal @DaveCarroll #customerservice
10:30am
Your dream could be your next best book. http://ow.ly/s2Qjo
Get the HootSuite Chrome extension to quickly schedule and share links, images and videos you visit on the web.
Install Extension
Jan 2, 11:01 am

15
LinkedIn

I would describe LinkedIn as purely a business networking site. It's the main floor coffee kiosk in a corporate tower. It is the Chamber of Commerce for the Internet. Name the business and executive level and find it in this network.

For example, if you are a copywriter who wants to work in a specified industry, you'll find the connections you need to propel your career in LinkedIn. If you are a singer and songwriter looking to press your first CD, you'll find a string of resources for recording studios, CD reproduction services, graphic design artists, concert hall managers, and music agents. If you are an author who pens books on business or any other industry, you will find qualified business leaders to interview.

While the free membership has some limits, it is still possible to connect with a very large group of people effectively.

One of the constraints to a LinkedIn membership is friending too many people. Yes, it does seem like an oxymoron for a social networking site. When using LinkedIn, be careful when you are looking for connections. Acquaintances you may have met in the past, may not remember you; if they hit the "I Don't Know" button (IDK) when choosing not to friend you, it penalizes you. If you amass enough IDK clicks, LinkedIn then insists you must have an email address before you can connect with anyone.

This is why the phrase LION shows up beside people's names in their profiles. It means LinkedIn Open Networker. You can connect with this person without any fear of him or her hitting the IDK button. It is an unwritten rule amongst open networkers. The person may decide not to accept the connection, but he or she will never hit the IDK.

I received a direct message from a LinkedIn connection I didn't really know. He asked me if he could introduce me to a fellow who was interested in publishing a book. The author turned out to be a doctor in China, who had just completed a book. After a few LinkedIn messages and emails, he hired me to produce his book. If I was not an open networker and chose not to accept the connection with the first fellow, I would not have been introduced to this project.

A nice feature on LinkedIn is being able to see which updates are the most popular. It's a good measuring tool to see how your content is doing.

LinkedIn lets you to set up your own group page and join others. Especially when you are first starting out, this is a good way to get to know people — by posting a topic of discussion and participating in other conversations. If a group ends up offering mostly spam and provides no value to you, leave the group.

1. Keep Active on LinkedIn

Many corporations and business professionals not quite sold on social networks will usually succumb to LinkedIn. They feel safe because it does not get too personal. Many jobs are posted on LinkedIn. In fact, there are some businesses that will only make their positions available through LinkedIn. I use LinkedIn as an online résumé and continually update it.

Do a regular audit of your LinkedIn profile to keep your information fresh. When you post daily, you show up in your connections' news feeds more, so more people notice you. Post at least one thing every day. The more information you put on your profile, the easier it is for people to decide if you are the person they are looking for.

People will discover you in the search options when they are looking for something in particular, such as a graphic designer, an accountant, or a movie producer. If your profile shows nothing, not even a photograph, chances are you won't get a second glance. People tend to make their decision about you based on your profile *before* they connect with you.

The Background section of your profile allows you to upload files, pictures, and videos. If you have YouTube videos or Power-Point presentations specific to the different areas on your résumé, add these buckets to provide more meat to your profile. Regularly editing these sections also helps keep your LinkedIn profile active and anything you do shows up in the Home feed for your connections to see.

One way of keeping your LinkedIn account active is to participate in the recommendations section. The recommendations can be used to stay in front of people's radar. It's a way to say, "Hey, I'm here and I see you." When you get a chance, return the favor to those who recommended you. Figure 49 pops up when you visit someone else's page.

Figure 49

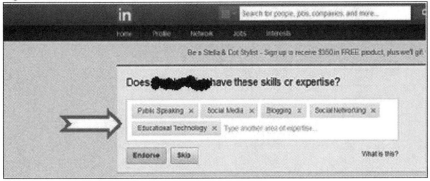

LinkedIn shows some categories (e.g., public speaking, social media, blogging) and asks if you would like to recommend a person. If you know some of these do not apply, you can delete them and only use the ones that apply, or add tasks you know that person does.

When you scroll down a profile you'll see a category of Skills & Endorsements; this is where those recommendations show up. Figure 50 shows the recommendations from my own LinkedIn profile. If someone has recommended you for the wrong task, it is okay to tell the person what you do.

Figure 50

16
Transmedia

"We all have the Gutenberg press in our pocket."

JEFF JARVIS
(BuzzMachine.com)

Transmedia is multi-platform storytelling that brings something human to an otherwise corporate sell. It taps into a primal need that most people want: To connect and have a sense of belonging.

If you can engage your audience with enthusiasm, they will spread your message willingly and you have a greater chance of capturing what you want from them than through a singular communications channel or by traditional methods.

A simple example is an advertisement for Kokanee beer. The company launched a series of television commercials involving a forest ranger and his assistant, and a Sasquatch that kept trying to steal their beer. This was during the early stages of social media, when brands hadn't really started to notice it yet.

The Kokanee Ranger story progressed to include three young, beautiful female ranger assistants and culminated when the viewers were asked to visit the website to log in and decide if the story continued — whether the ranger lived or died.[1] Once the viewer logged in and chose the ranger's fate, they could see a video of what their story ending would look like.

This book and a blog post[2] I wrote added two more platforms that spread the Kokanee brand messages. Fans of this commercial series produced their own videos[3] to add to the media.

1. Transmedia through Television and Movies

In 2010, the Producers Guild of America named "transmedia producer" an official title. "A Transmedia Producer credit is given to the person(s) responsible for a significant portion of a project's long-term planning, development, production, and/or maintenance of narrative continuity across multiple platforms, and creation of original storylines for new platforms."[4] To qualify for transmedia, there have to be three or more narrative storylines within the same fictional universe.

Transmedia is a natural fit for television shows. It is a way to expand on and engage viewers long after each episode ends. The ultimate goal is to turn viewers into disciples who spread their enthusiasm about the show across the Web in order to attract more viewers.

Mad Men is a classic example. There is extra narrative about each show on the website. The conversation gets spread a number of ways. When you visit the landing page, there is a sign-up box to join the *Mad Men* Social Club.

Sections like *Mad Men* Talk tap into the idea that fans love to talk about their favorite show and its characters. This feedback also gives a show's producers insight into how they might direct the storyline for future episodes.

The Cocktail Culture App is another way to embed the show into a fan's everyday experience. This app shows people how to make the classic drinks their favorite characters make on the show.

1 "Kokanee Ranger Live or Die," YouTube.com, accessed July 7, 2014.
  www.youtube.com/watch?v=xrehBj8gowk
2 "Transmedia Storytelling Sells Beer," The Publishing Dashboard, accessed July 7, 2014.
  http://publishingdashboard.blogspot.ca/2013/01/transmedia-storytelling-sells-beer.html
3 "A Tribute to Kokanee Ranger's Horrible Fate," YouTube.com, accessed July 7, 2014.
  http://youtu.be/MY6PcCKOfww
4 "PGA: Transmedia Producers Have Arrived," *Filmmaker Magazine*, accessed July 7, 2014.
  http://filmmakermagazine.com/6673-pga-transmedia-producers-have-arrived/#.U3VKvSgXJfR

The show also adds unique content to its Facebook page. On Twitter, you'll find fans talking about the show before, during, and after an episode and season have aired. The conversation scroll is fast and furious during a show.

The buzz that can be generated prior to the release of a production can accelerate beyond a person's expectations. But you also need imagination and creative genius to pull it off.

There are a couple of blazing examples of this. The television show *Dexter* created a successful campaign that gathered a community of viewers strongly invested in the *Dexter* brand and its characters.[5] There were clues unveiled by new tasks that led to exclusive previews and recordings. The launch was closely tied to the San Diego Comic-Con and involved a mobile game, a real game, scavenger hunt, a crowdsourced investigation led by a former FBI agent, puzzle solving, an eBay bidding war, and unique content created by fans.

The Dark Knight Rises movie crossed both digital and real world communities in its transmedia marketing campaign and tapped into more than 10 million participants in more than 75 countries and hundreds of web pages.[6] When the movie finally opened at the box office, it was the top grossing film on opening day. The campaign included an alternate reality game, mobile phones, print, email, live events, exclusive video, and collectibles. It even spilled onto news anchors' desks.

Clues to kickstart the scavenger hunt were launched at San Diego Comic-Con. *The Dark Knight* community appeared at local landmarks in full Joker makeup. There were robocalls made by the character Harvey Dent to mobilize people into the streets to take back Gotham City. The result: Worldwide box office receipts alone totaled well more than a billion dollars.

2. Creating Awareness through Transmedia

Success isn't always about money. It will differ with each campaign. It could be about awareness, creating a community of raving fans, or spreading good deeds.

---

5 "Dexter Transmedia Case Study by Modernista! & Showtime ... via Jawbone TV," YouTube.com, accessed July 7, 2014.
www.youtube.com/watch?v=Pp1_69jfbs8&list=PLkGyRMp0aLb99V3mtHO5G02TExcropjYZ&feature=share&index=3
6 "Dark Knight-Viral Marketing Campaign," YouTube.com, accessed July 7, 2014.
www.youtube.com/watch?v=VpuC7HhCPWA&feature=share&list=PLkGyRMp0aLb99V3mtHO502TExcropjYZ&index=4

Children's Prize[7] ran a contest to award a $1 million prize to the person or organization that could save the most children aged five and younger. The message was spread across various digital platforms to task the global community with becoming altruistic social media agents to find inventors of hope.

The Children's Prize campaign was spearheaded by engineer Dr. Ted Caplow, whose background in renewable energy, sustainable food production, and water contaminants made him ever aware that saving children meant saving communities.

A team of judges, including those from Harvard School of Public Health and the University of Miami Department of Pediatrics helped select eight finalists from the 565 proposals received from 70 countries. These finalists presented approaches to accelerating a reduction in child mortality rates. The 2013 winner was Dr. Anita Zaidi, who introduced a package of proven interventions in maternal, newborn, and child health to an impoverished fishing village in Karachi, Pakistan, which would save at least 165 lives.

In 2009, Oprah Winfrey created a media event[8] that you could call early transmedia. It was a webcast for the Oprah Book Club, featuring a one-on-one interview with Uwen Akpan, the author of *Say You're One of Them*, a collection of stories about family and life in Africa.

The webcast featured Anderson Cooper interview vignettes, a live Facebook feed, Skype questions from the readers, and more. Diving deeper into this event, some of its elements included:

- Videos of charitable ventures by celebrities in Africa.

- Online article about author.

- Excerpt of the book.

- Interactive map of Africa.

- Discussion group.

- Feedback section.

- Video blog.

- Oprah discussing on video why this book was selected.

---

7 Children's Prize, accessed July 7, 2014. http://ChildrensPrize.org
8 "Oprah's Book Club, *Say You're One of Them* Webcast," Oprah.com, accessed July 7, 2014. www.oprah.com/oprahsbookclub/Watch-Oprahs-Book-Club-Say-Youre-One-of-Them-Webcast-Video

- Video about the author, including personal topics.

- Stories about Africa.

- Other people that the author has inspired in audio and video.

- Running video blog.

- How to get involved with helping Africa.

- Transcript of webcast.

3. Design Your Own Transmedia Campaign

Transmedia storytelling taps into a primal need that most people want: To connect and have a sense of belonging. If you can engage customers with enthusiasm, they will spread your message willingly and you have a greater chance of capturing what you want from them than through a singular communications channel or by traditional methods.

This section will help you design your own unique transmedia campaign. There are a few resources I'd first like to share with you that will open up your creative genius. While I have not used their words verbatim, many of the tips below were culled from people such as Robert Pratten, founder of Transmedia Storyteller; TEDxTransmedia; Transmedia LA, and Terribleminds. I tweet their posts daily through a paper.li newspaper: *The Transmedia Tribune.*

As you begin to brainstorm ideas, consider the following questions:

- Story: What is the story behind the media?

- Experience: What is the audience experience going to be?

- Premise: What is the gist of the entire project?

- Audience: Where will you find your viewers, readers, or listeners?

- Platforms: What platforms will you incorporate? (See the end of this section for a list of platforms to consider.)

The story is the narrative, and the story intercepts the real world by integrating real locations, times, people, and events. It is cocreated by its audience's ability to change or add to the narrative. In the

Dexter narrative, the story — the launch of the new season — was intercepted by games, treasure hunts, and other interactive activities in which the viewers had to participate to see special previews and learn more about what to expect with the show. The audience drove the process forward with their joining in, but ultimately at the end, at a live event, it was the audience that determined how that story ended, when two characters faced off against each other.

Interactive game mechanics help the audience reach its goal to find and help write the story. The use of gamification (taking aspects of a video game and bringing them to life) is a worthy component of successful transmedia campaigns.

Gamification entails rewarding players (i.e., audience, users) for activities. Typical game rewards are points, badges, and levels. In the case of the *Dexter* game, participants were given another video or audio clue after the completion of a task (finding a lead or conducting a number of kills in a video game). Leader boards and virtual progress bars help fuel engagement. Game developers know that competition, achievement, status, self-expression, and benevolence all play into a person's natural desires.

You may want to design something similar to Figure 51 as you brainstorm your ideas. The "core story" in the center of Figure 51 is your message. From there it can be spread to different media to paint the full picture.

Use a spreadsheet or another format that you are comfortable with while planning your transmedia campaign. How you organize the script will probably differ from the next person, much like writing a manuscript. We all have our own filing systems.

Break down the different elements:

- What is the time line for each platform and the entire project? For example, the *Dexter* campaign needed a time line for participants to reach the final event or else the game could continue on indefinitely.

- How do you vary the uses of each platform to create different directions of the story?

- How does each platform address the different types of audiences?

Figure 51

- Where is the story going? In the Batman campaign, the purpose was to get the audience interested and be part of the story in order to generate ticket sales at the theater when the movie opened. The *Dexter* campaign intended to get viewers watching the new season. For more real-life campaign examples, check out Transmedia Storyteller's list of case studies.[9]

Dig deeper into each element:

- Why does the story need that platform?
- How does the platform create engagement?
- Is it building a community? How?
- Does it generate revenue or awareness?

Get your audience involved in telling the story; this may mean rewriting the ending. Leave part of the story unsaid so the audience will get to finish it.

Consider all platforms and how you can connect them with your transmedia campaign:

- Twitter

9 "Art and ARGs," Transmedia Storyteller, accessed July 7, 2014.
   www.tstoryteller.com/case-study-categories/arts-and-args

- LinkedIn
- Facebook
- YouTube
- Website
- SlideShare
- Newspaper
- Television
- Radio
- Billboards
- Magnetic truck signs
- Bus signs
- Baseball outfield advertising
- Novelties
- Clothing
- Apps
- Events
- Books
- Magazines
- Audiobooks
- Ebooks
- Merchandising
- Texting
- Radio
- Product labels

When it comes to transmedia campaigns, you can go big or small and everything in between. It all comes down to creativity and time.

17
Public Relations

"Ten years ago, we got the information from the company. Now we're going to get the truth."

SETH GODIN

Vocus publishes an annual "State of the Media Report," and since 2009, there has been a downward spiral in traditional media. The 2010 report showed:[1]

- Approximately 293 newspapers folded.

- Eight magazines with a circulation of 1 million or more ceased publication.

- Including print and online versions, a total of 1,126 magazines closed.

- Radio stations lost more than 10,000 jobs.

More than 100 (US) TV stations were affected by their parent companies filing for Chapter 11 bankruptcy.

---

1 "2010 State of the Media: An Analysis of the Changing Media Landscape by the Vocus Media Research Team," SlideShare, accessed July 7, 2014. www.slideshare.net/Vocus/vocus-2010-stateofthemedia

For the most part, traditional media shunned social media back then. The ability to communicate directly with the audience made many reporters uncomfortable.

Fast forward to 2013 and the story has changed dramatically. While media outlets are still in trouble, they have synergized social media into their day-to-day structure. Reporters use social media to monitor the pulse of their viewership, readership, and/or listenership. Facebook and Twitter are the media's main platforms; they are used to push out supplementary content and to build on their individual brands.

The *2013 Vocus State of the Media* report showed:[2]

- 128 newspapers folded.

- More than 900 patch sites were gutted (aggregator of local news and sources).

- 150 magazines closed, although 97 new publications were launched (59 of them in print).

- Mobile devices ruled.

- Acquisitions, relaunches, and consolidations were commonplace.

1. Old Media Rules Still Apply

While it is possible to spread a message through social networks and other Internet-based web platforms, a blended approach, using both digital and traditional media, offers a better reach.

Pitching the media still has its rules, much like before social media, in that the structure of a press release is still the same, you still use media advisories to invite reporters to events, and public service announcements are still used to shed light on issues that affect the public.

The media may converse with you in social media, but that is not where they want you to pitch your story to reporters. Email is still the preferred mechanism. However, if you use an online press release service, reporters will still be able to pick it up.

The one thing that will kill any media pitch is bad grammar and spelling. If you can't take the time to edit your message and

2 "Vocus' State of the Media 2013 Report: The Social Transformations," accessed July 78, 2014. www.vocus.com/blog/state-of-the-media-report-2013/

make it look professional, you won't be taken seriously and your message will be lost without any chance of being revived. Literacy counts in all aspects of the web.

2. The Media Landscape

"News media is no longer in control of its own future."

CHRIS BROGAN

Because the mainstream media industry is changing, public relations departments have to rethink their priority hierarchy when it comes to media importance. They can no longer afford to "dis" the electronic media. That doesn't mean accrediting every Tom, Dick, and Jane who has a blog or website, but some blogs and independent media sites do wield a powerful voice and/or come with huge followings.

When the media has a problem or fails to engage with its audience, the audience spreads the word to its own networks. If a media outlet has nobody tasked with monitoring the social networks, then there is no response, and issues tend to culminate and result in a trending hashtag, such as #nbcfail that went viral during the 2012 Olympic Winter Games.[3]

A tweet unheard is much like calling your cable company for Internet support and nobody answering the phone.

One place where the traditional media tends to fail dramatically is in its race to be the first to break a story. Before Twitter, reporters had time to vet their sources and include a couple of interviews before breaking the news.

Today, the story goes viral on Twitter before it sees the light of an editor's desk. In their rush to beat the social network, the media has risked citizens' reputations and lives by getting the story wrong. An example of this is all the misinformation around the Boston Marathon bombings in 2013.[4] When it happens so frequently with such an absence of acumen, credibility dies and that station, reporter, and maybe all media, is no longer considered a viable news source.

3 "#nbcfail economics," Jeff Jarvis on Google+, accessed July 7, 2014.
  https://plus.google.com/+JeffJarvis/posts/1uwNFQKJ7ra
4 "Boston Bombings Reveal Media Full of Mistakes, False Reports (VIDEO)," The Huffington Post, accessed July 7, 2014.
  www.huffingtonpost.com/2013/04/22/boston-bombings-media-mistakes_n_3135105.html

There is another element that has infiltrated North American and European national media outlets: News is no longer about news but rather it is about ratings. It is why you see the most salacious story discussed the most, even if it has nothing to do with a national audience.

There is also the aspect of the media not wanting to create waves and risk their accreditation. At least there is suspicion over this when one sees softball questions from reporters, instead of the tough ones that make people squirm in their seat. For an example of this, see "Steve Kroft's Softball Obama Interviews Diminish '60 Minutes'" by Conor Friedersdorf.[5]

Because news organizations have to answer to shareholders, in lieu of hemorrhaging profits, they've closed down foreign bureaus, laid off reporters, and instead pooled news stories from far-off locations. You see the same story being reported with the same angle on nearly every network. Even local stories suffer.

If there are no reporters covering stories, the only media is social media.

3. User-Generated Content

"The Internet is to the news today what TV was to the newspaper."

JEFF JARVIS

User-generated content is not about the stereotypical blogger in the basement. Citizen journalists fill the gap for media outlets in every location. Some of the biggest breaking stories worldwide began on Twitter, reported by citizen journalists, and in countries with no access to Western media.

On June 20, 2009, a young woman, Neda Agha-Soltan, was gunned down in the streets of Tehran, Iran, during a protest. Her death was captured on video and it didn't take long for it to go viral across social media.[6]

Agha-Soltan became the face of a demonstration against election results in Iran. Of course, there was no media coverage at the

---

5 "Steve Kroft's Softball Obama Interviews Diminish '60 Minutes," The Atlantic.com, accessed July 7, 2014.
  www.theatlantic.com/politics/archive/2013/01/steve-krofts-softball-obama-interviews-diminish-60-minutes/272611/
6 "Death of Neda Agha-Soltan," Wikipedia.org, accessed July 7, 2014.
  http://en.wikipedia.org/wiki/Death_of_Neda_Agha-Soltan

time of her death, but it became a big enough story that couldn't be ignored. News outlets began following the demonstrations and used the video and pictures uploaded by Iranian citizens to Twitter and Facebook (who use proxy servers for anonymity). News anchors and reporters were quick to report that none of the material could be verified. Still, they used the information because they were the only images coming out of that country.

About a year and a half later, the Arab Spring was born, which was a wave of demonstrations and protests in Arab countries.[7] You saw similar protocol by news media, who were slow, if at all able, to get reporters to Bahrain or Egypt.

Mainstream television media outlets know their limitations for boots-on-the-ground reporting, so nearly all have reached out to viewers to help them find stories, and most important, video footage. Enter tools such as the CNN iReport. This section of the CNN website asks viewers to submit their video and stories in their own words, but the iReport Toolkit[8] is a checklist of what makes a good story.

7 "Arab Spring," Wikipedia.org, accessed July 7, 2014. http://en.wikipedia.org/wiki/Arab_Spring
8 "iReport Toolkit," CNN.com, accessed July 7, 2014. http://ireport.cnn.com/toolkit.jspa

Conclusion

"If you're not prepared to do business in a totally different way, then you're wasting your time and your money in trying to turn the Internet into TV 2.0."

SETH GODIN

All media from this point forward must fit into a mobile device. Positioning for the future means television, radio, books, and news must adapt to, conform with, and become ever-changing technology.

As platforms and products develop, there are common denominators that will make or break their success: convenience, mobility, accessibility, and fast loading.

If the most remote village locations in central Africa can have access to Facebook, no marketer in North America has an excuse to be unconnected.[1]

---

1 "Connecting Africa — Bringing e-learning to remote villages," SOS Children's Villages, accessed July 7, 2014. www.sos-childrensvillages.org/news-and-stories/news/connecting-africa

It boils down to these questions:

- Who are you in business for?
- Why should anyone read your book, blog, or website?
- How will you reach your audience or customers?
- Are you positioned for the future?
- Are you engaged with your audience?
- How do you get someone excited about what you are doing?
- When is the last time you did a cyber-audit on yourself?

Whether or not our educational system has caught up with what people are actually doing to communicate and publish does not mean you can afford to ignore these changes.

In 2014, Lorde was nominated for four Grammy Awards and won two: Song of the Year ("Royals") and Best Pop Solo Performance. Lorde signed with Universal at age 13 and posted "The Love Club" on SoundCloud in November 2012 as a free download. By the time 60,000 clicked through, the record company stepped in to intervene. The song "Royals" was added to Spotify and became the most streamed song in New Zealand, thus launching Lorde as 2013's most viral new artist worldwide. Her success was organic — through social media.

On a side note, 11 months after "Royals" (US Version) was uploaded to the LordeVEVO YouTube channel, it had received 268,927,667 views.

Unlike Lorde, Macklemore and Ryan Lewis didn't have a label when they released their single "Thrift Shop." It went to number one on the US Billboard Hot 100. The last time a song reached number one without the support of a label was Lisa Loeb's "Stay (I Missed You)" in 1994.

When "Can't Hold Us" made number one, Macklemore and Ryan Lewis became the first duo with two singles to top the chart. Social media and video-sharing websites were the impetus that moved the duo to stardom. They were awarded the YouTube Breakthrough award at the inaugural YouTube Music Awards in 2013, then they were nominated for seven 2014 Grammy Awards.

They took home four: Best New Artist, Best Rap Album (*The Heist*), Best Rap Song, and Best Rap Performance ("Thrift Shop").

Music isn't the only creative venture to enjoy success via social media. There are numerous examples of social media accounts that turned into books, such as *Sh*t My Dad Says*.[2]

When Justin Halpern opened up a Twitter account @shitmydadsays, he was a semi-employed comic writer. His posts became an overnight success. That simple Twitter account blossomed into a *New York Times* bestselling book and a television series starring William Shatner.

Social media tools are available to everyone — teenagers, professional marketers, authors, musicians, corporations, publishers, and governments. The playing field is level and the one that shines on top is the one who put in the right attitude and effort.

The one key takeaway from everything you've read in this book should be that *you* control your own success.

---

2 "IZ Social Media Accounts That Turned into Books," Mashable.com. accessed July 7, 2014. http://mashable.com/2013/12/08/social-media-book-deals/